When You're Running Empty

CINDI McMENAMIN

HARVEST HOUSE PUBLISHERS

EUGENE, OREGON

Cover by Koechel Peterson & Associates, Inc., Minneapolis, Minnesota

Cover photo © Jack Hollingsworth/Blend Images/Getty Images

WHEN YOU'RE RUNNING ON EMPTY
Copyright © 2006 by Cindi McMenamin
Published by Harvest House Publishers
Eugene, Oregon 97402

Library of Congress Cataloging-in-Publication Data
McMenamin, Cindi, 1965-
    When you're running on empty / Cindi McMenamin.
        p. cm.
    Includes bibliographical references.
    ISBN-13: 978–0-7369–1749–0 (pbk.)
    ISBN-10: 0–7369–1749–7
    1. Christian women—Religious life. 2. Christian women—Health and hygiene. I. Title.
    BV4527.M4335 2006
    248.8'43—dc22   2005031497

Printed in the United States of America

06 07 08 09 10 11 12 13 14 / DP-MS / 10 9 8 7 6 5 4 3 2 1

*For every woman who has ever felt worn out
and run down...especially in ministry.
My prayer is that through this book you will be
encouraged to not grow weary in doing good.*

Galatians 6:9

Acknowledgments

Special thanks to…

- My editor, Steve Miller, at Harvest House Publishers, for praying for me and encouraging me when I feel I'm running on empty.

- Paul, Scott, and the team at Powerhouse Gym Murrieta (California) for your commitment to health and fitness…and for the most fun (and frustration) I've had in my life—getting that club up and running!

- Holly Galloway, my Jazzercise® instructor, for keeping me from running on empty by making fitness fun!

- Chris and Diane—my "good company" and my good friends.

- My daughter, Dana, for keeping me on my toes and keeping a song in her heart.

- My husband, Hugh, for helping me "refuel" every Friday.

- And, above all, my gratitude goes to the Lord Jesus Christ, who "emptied Himself" for me so that I could experience life with Him. May my life be willingly emptied out for You over and over again.

Contents

Finding a Way to Refuel 7

Part I: Keeping Focus

1. Start Your Day with Prayer 15
2. Refuel with God's Word 23
3. Know Whom You're Trying to Please 29
4. Serve Out of Inspiration, Not Obligation 37
5. Invest in What's Eternal 43
6. Act on Facts, Not Feelings 49
7. Determine Whom You'll Trust 59

Part II: Keeping Fit

8. Keep a Clean Heart 69
9. Keep Good Company 77
10. Keep a Healthy Diet 83
11. Keep Moving 91
12. Keep Your Sleep 99
13. Keep at It 105

Part III: Keeping Fresh

14. Find Your Hideaway 115
15. In All Things Sing 121
16. Simplify the Day 125
17. Take Time to Play 131
18. Take Time to Reflect 137

19. Get Outdoors. 143

20. Find the View 149

21. Regain the Wonder 153

22. Re-ignite the Flame. 161

      Welcome to a New Way of Life 169

      Appendix: Praying Through the Psalms 171

      Notes 174

Finding a Way to Refuel

I know how you feel.

Life seems to be going in a million different directions. There are so many things for you to do in so little time. Kids are pulling at you, or your job is pushing you. Responsibilities abound. And there's only one of you.

I, too, know what it's like to feel as though you're running on empty.

I'm not sure when it happened. It must have been a gradual process. But the day I realized I was feeling drained and defeated, I knew something was wrong. I'd lost my fire, my fervor, my fuel.

I'd written books on letting God meet your emotional needs, yet emotionally I was empty. I wrote about how God strengthens us through our alone times but I was feeling weakened. I'd written a book on how to truly rest and I was feeling more overwhelmed than ever. And a year earlier I'd written a book on discovering and living out your dream and yet I was struggling with a lack of motivation.

What was wrong with me? Why was I feeling so complacent? Why did I have no motivation to continue forward?

I met with a doctor-friend of mine and his wife over lunch one day and talked about it.

"Burnout manifests itself in a certain activity you're doing to the point that you've emptied the battery out," said Dr. Jeff Birchall, who sees a new person dealing with some sort of exhaustion, anxiety, or depression every day...and follows up with about four every day.

Dr. Birchall said 50 percent of all people suffer from burnout at some point in their life, 10 percent at any given moment.

The symptoms of burnout? They sound a lot like the symptoms of running on empty:

- chronic fatigue (exhaustion, tiredness, a sense of being physically run down)
- difficulty sleeping (waking in the middle of the night and finding yourself unable to return to sleep)
- decreased concentration (can't finish things)
- anger at those making demands
- self-criticism for putting up with the demands
- cynicism, negativity, and irritability
- a sense of being besieged
- exploding easily at seemingly inconsequential things
- frequent headaches and stomachaches
- changes in appetite resulting in weight loss or gain
- shortness of breath
- increased irritability (men tend to get angry more; women tend to cry more)
- social withdrawal
- depression
- feelings of helplessness[1]

Maybe you can relate to some of those symptoms. Burnout can sometimes look like depression. Sometimes like anxiety. Some of us feel just a hint of it, as if we're merely getting our toes wet...and others of us are drowning in it.

I knew I wasn't in a state of depression. I wasn't suffering from anxiety. But I was tired, overwhelmed, and frustrated. The fire of my relationship with God that once burned brightly now seemed to be barely flickering. The juices had dried up. The motivation was lost. I was running on empty.

My friend says some cases of burnout or exhaustion require medication. Some require counseling. And many of the cases require a change of environment to get the balance they need in their life. That one was mine. I needed the balance. Too much striving, not enough trusting. Too much work, not enough rest. Too much expenditure, not enough filling. It was time for something to change.

I went to the Psalms—Scripture's songs of human emotion—and related to the songwriters. They, too, experienced seasons of weariness and emptiness. They, too, cried out for help. And I began to notice a link between their cries for help while flat on their faces, and their ability to get back up on their feet again. What I saw in there, as that link, was a shift in focus (following times of prayer and praise) and a sense of determination.

The psalmists often sang—in their songs of frustration and desperation—the words "I will" when it came to getting out of their slump.

Asaph, in Psalm 77, was disillusioned with the way life was going. But he said, "*I will meditate* on all Thy works...*I will remember* your deeds."[2]

David, in asking God to consider his sighing and hear his cries for help, said, "*I will come* into your house; in reverence *will I bow down*" (Psalm 5:7). And when he felt like he was being defeated, he said "*I will know* that God is for me...*I will* not be afraid" (Psalm 56:9–11).

The psalmists didn't say, "I think" or, "I feel" or, "I should." It was, "I *will*." They expressed a sense of determination. In all 150 psalms in the Bible, the phrase "I will" is sung at least 140 times. That told me something. It made me realize that whether I feel empty or not, whether I am motivated or not, I need to *do* something to allow God to infuse energy into my life again. I needed to take whatever action would put me in the place where God could relight the fire in me and re-ignite the passion that once burned brightly. And I couldn't simply sit and wait until I *felt* like doing something, because the feeling might never come.

So I began to *will* to start my day right by starting it with prayer, to keep myself focused, to act on fact rather than feelings, to keep a clean heart, and to keep at whatever else God called me to. And as I began to follow a course of action, God met me where I was and infused that fuel back into my life.

I imagine you know what it's like to trudge through the day feeling you have little left to give. You, too, probably feel like you have too many obligations, too much stress, not enough energy. You feel as if you have no fuel, no fire, no way to get through the day. But you don't have to run on empty anymore.

In this book I want to share with you, chapter by chapter, how to rise above the feelings of listlessness and recharge, refuel, and replenish. I plan to do that by sharing with you the "I will" course of action that brought me—and will hopefully bring you—to that well for the life-giving water and energy-inducing fuel that you need. I can't guarantee it will happen at the same speed and in the same way that it did with me. I can't even guarantee the suggestions I offer in this book will work for you. But *God* works. He designed us and He knows how to carefully pick us up, renew us, and get us going again. And as you begin to focus on God, and get your mind, body, and soul in the place where He can meet you, He'll get to work on what's left of you, mending you to whole-ness and efficiency once again.

I will share with you practical ways that pick me—and others—up when we're too low to go any lower and too fried to go any further. We'll look at keeping focus (with your mind), keeping fit (with your body), and keeping fresh (with your soul). So that as we find ourselves renewed, we'll not only be able to soar...we'll be able to help energize others as well.

As I share with you what I had to "will" to do each and every morning, keep in mind this is not so much a book on willpower—but on "His power"—the power that our Maker infuses into us when we come to Him and seek to live the way He intended for us to live. It's a book about keeping focus, keeping fit, and keeping fresh by keeping our lives centered on Him and balanced as a whole.

So...will you give Him the burned-out remnants of your life and let Him restore the passion, re-ignite the flame, and refuel your soul?

For all the days you've wished there was a well you could go to for the energy you needed to get through the day...for all the times you've wished there was a quick fix from something pure and simple...take heart. Such a well exists. And it's not very difficult to get there.

Come, my friend...it's time to refuel, refresh, and relish your God-given life again.

Part I:
Keeping Focus

I am focusing all my energies on this one thing: Forgetting the past and looking forward to what lies ahead, I strain to reach the end of the race and receive the prize...

PHILIPPIANS 3:13–14 NLT

Feeling run down is not just a physical thing. Attitude is everything. And we are what we believe. How we start our day, what we fuel ourselves with, who we're trying to please, why we do what we're doing, how we respond to our feelings, and who we're ultimately trusting all contribute to whether we're feeling determined and motivated to get it done, or whether we're dragging our feet and feeling we can't make it through the day. A good solid focus will fuel you, mentally, through what lies ahead and keep you from running on empty.

It all starts with keeping focus...

Chapter 1

Start Your Day with Prayer

In the morning, O LORD, you hear my voice;
in the morning I lay my requests before you
and wait in expectation.
PSALM 5:3

If you're like me, you'd rather just sleep in every morning. I wasn't always that way. I remember days in my early thirties when I eagerly rose from bed at 5:30 AM, spent some precious time in prayer and Bible study, and then showered and got on with an extremely productive day.

Where did *those* days go?

Now that I'm past 40, it's not nearly as easy to rise and shine and conquer like I used to. Seems like there's this added weight of obligations, age, physical wear and tear, and, sometimes, just plain weight!

I'd just as soon let the snooze alarm go off a few times and lay in bed thinking about what I'd do if I just had a little more energy. That's where the self-discipline comes in. I know, in my heart of hearts, that if I'm self-disciplined, from the time I get up I'll be much less sluggish and far more productive. That's where the "will" comes in—the will to start the day right.

> God has a way of honoring our time and helping us be more productive in our day when we first honor Him.

As I lie in bed, I must remember that the day was not created for me and whatever I want to do. There's Someone Else in the picture. And what is His idea of why I was given one more day?

The Westminster Confession says, "The chief end of man is to glorify God and enjoy Him forever." You and I were created for relationship with the living God. That's an amazing concept well worth thinking about. In fact, when I remember to focus on that concept as soon as I wake up, it's enough to get me out of bed knowing that my Creator is waiting to enjoy the day with me. If it were the other way around, I'd probably wait till I felt like being with God. But He is always waiting for me…and for you. And who are *we* to make the God of the Universe wait?

Finding Your Focus

The apostle Paul said in Philippians 3:13–14, "This *one thing* I do: Forgetting what is behind and straining toward what is ahead, I press on…." What did he *press on* toward? The prize—the relationship with God. In spite of life's many obligations and pressures, he knew the *one thing* he needed to do was to keep his relationship with God a priority.

When you first wake up and contemplate your day, can you, too, ask yourself, "What is the *one thing* I must do today?"

Maybe your answer is "I must take care of my children." Or, "I must get that project completed." Maybe it's even "I must get through this day."

Yet God tells us in the Bible "and [God] will give you all you need from day to day if you live for him and make the Kingdom of God your primary concern" (Matthew 6:33 NLT). Know the *one thing* you must do today (put your relationship with God first), and everything else will fall into place.

I've found this true in my life time and time again. When I take the time to start my day off right—by rising a little earlier so I have time to quiet my heart and talk to God—I am able to focus first and foremost on the *one thing*. Then all the other things I need to do fall amazingly into place.

God has a way of honoring our time and helping us be more productive in our day when we first honor Him. And by taking to Him all that we have to do that day, we are also releasing it to His control, which removes from us the weight and burden of feeling we have to control all the day's events.

The Bible also says, "Give all your worries and cares to God, for he cares about what happens to you."[1] There is a tremendous amount of refreshment that comes from handing over to God—early in the day—all that concerns us and weighs us down. Then He fills us with His peace so we can face the day without anxiety.

God knows we're prone to becoming stressed out about things. That's why He told us in His Word, "Don't worry about anything; instead, pray about everything. Tell God what you need, and thank him for all he has done. If you do this, you will experience God's peace, which is far more wonderful than the human mind can understand. His peace will guard your hearts and minds as you live in Christ Jesus."[2]

Hiding Away with God

King David, who was evidently stressed and run down at times, said, "The *one thing* I ask of the LORD—the thing I seek most—is to live in the house of the LORD all the days of my life, delighting in the LORD's perfections and meditating in his Temple. For he will conceal me there when troubles come; he will hide me in his sanctuary. He will place me out of reach on a high rock." [3]

David was saying that of all the things he could have (and for a king, not too much is out of reach!), he wanted a hideaway with God— a place where he'd be concealed, hidden, *out of reach* from trouble. He found that place by meditating on the Lord, seeking His face, finding that quiet time to focus on God.

David also found that time in the morning. As busy as he was— running the kingdom of Israel, commander-in-chief of Israel's army, husband to several wives, father to several children (and many of them quite dysfunctional)—he experienced stress at times. In one song he wrote, "Oh, how I wish I had wings like a dove; then I would fly away and rest! I would fly far away to the quiet of the wilderness. How quickly I would escape—far away from this wild storm…."[4] Yes, David apparently faced stress and burnout, and at times must have felt he was running on empty. Yet we find throughout his songs some references to getting away with God in the morning, and starting his day right… with prayer.

"Listen to my voice in the morning, LORD," David sang. "Each morning I bring my request to you and wait expectantly" (Psalm 5:3 NLT).

Can you meet with God for a few minutes each morning and therefore start your day right? Can you prayerfully reflect on His Word in order to compose your thoughts and prioritize your day? Can you remember that, above all things, your relationship with God is why you're here? When that relationship is humming along, so will all the other aspects of your life.

By starting your day in quiet reflection and prayer, you are opening the channels of communication with God that will remain open throughout the day. You are ushering peace into your day, and keeping chaos from crashing into it.

Making It Happen

If you don't already have a regular plan of starting your day with prayer, here's one that has worked for me:

1. *Find a quiet place to retreat to every morning.* Do you have a "sanctuary" to which you can hide away with God? It doesn't need to be fancy...just a place where you can get away from the distractions of the morning and meet quietly with God. For example, one of my friends goes into her walk-in closet and closes the door. Maybe your place of retreat is early in the morning at the kitchen table, while the house is still quiet and before you open the newspaper. It may be your living room chair by the window, after the kids leave for school. Or it may be in your car—with the radio turned off—while you're driving to work. Find that place and make it your "sanctuary"—a regular meeting place with God. (I'll talk more in-depth about finding your "hideaway" in chapter 14.)

2. *Focus your mind in quiet prayer.* Once you've found your sanctuary, ask God to help you quiet your mind and focus your thoughts on Him. Then ask God what He'd like of you that day, rather than telling God what you want from Him. Open your Bible to a psalm and pray through it. As you do this, your prayers become guided by God and you end up seeking His will, not

your own, for the day. Therein lies the peace and the power and the fuel to get through the day. (See page 171 for instructions on "Praying Through the Psalms.")

3. *Follow God's still, quiet voice throughout the day.* As you open the channels of communication with God in the morning, through prayer, you will be placing yourself on the "receiving end" of what He wants to say to you throughout the day. Listening for God's still, quiet voice throughout the day tunes your ears to what He wants to say and keeps you in a "quiet mode" throughout the day. This will protect you from running the pace that makes you feel you're running on empty.[5] If you can quiet your heart first thing in the morning, then keep that quiet heart throughout the day, then you will have found a way to carry your "sanctuary" with you throughout the day and stay in a restful, quiet mode.

So, are you ready to start your day right? Those three action steps, on a daily basis, will get you out of the habit of running harried and shift you into a slower mode of *walking* enjoyably *through* your day so you don't find yourself *running* on empty at the *end* of the day.

Pick-Me-Up Prayer

Lord, You call me when I first arise. And how I want to be there when You call, meeting You like the dawn meets the morning sky. How many times have You waited, only for me to not show up? I don't want to be a no-show any longer.

Wake me gently and prompt me to a place where I can get alone with You while the house still sleeps. Help me to sit quietly as You bring Your rest into my soul. Remind me of the *one thing* that is most important. The one thing *You* want from me is written all over Your Word. You say You love me with an everlasting love (Jeremiah 31:3). You want me to live with hope and purpose (Jeremiah 29:11). And You paid the ultimate price on the cross to secure me as Your own.

May I, like David, sing in my heart, "There is one thing that I want…and it's You—to know You, to commune with You, to enjoy You forever." Give me the strength and energy to prove it by getting out of bed every morning and spending the first part of my day in prayer with You. From now on when You call in the morning, may I already be waiting for You…

My soul waits for the Lord,
more than watchmen wait for the morning…

(PSALM 130:6).

Chapter 2

Refuel with God's Word

The law of the LORD is perfect, reviving the soul.
PSALM 19:7

...I will not neglect your word.
PSALM 119:16

Ever have one of those mini-vacations where you take a couple days to sit by the hotel pool, or enjoy a stay on a houseboat or spend a few days in the mountains? And then as soon as you returned to your everyday routine, you found that your sense of relaxation and rest disappeared quickly? That's because you got away for a temporary fix. To keep from running on empty, you need a lasting one.

When I went on a cruise with my family a few summers ago, I was stress-free in terms of my schedule and all that I felt I needed to get done.

I took the downtime and enjoyed quiet meals on the ship, shopped at exotic ports of call, snorkeled in crystal-clear water, and laid on the white sands of the Caribbean. But when I got back home, I found that I was still hardly motivated to get back to work. That's because while I was gone I may have been resting and relaxing, but I wasn't refueling.

> When I'm running on empty, I now ask myself how long it's been since I've refueled from the Word.

About a month after the cruise, I vacationed with my family and some friends for a week at a lake. During that week away, I took morning walks in the peaceful outdoors, sat on the deck of the cabin in the evenings and read, did some strenuous water skiing (and more strenuous wipeouts in the water) and even learned to drive a boat! But that week was different than the cruise. I came back home refreshed. That's because I made sure, while at the lake, that I was refueling. I had taken the time to get into God's Word and let Him pour His fuel into my life.

Psalm 19 says that God's Word is "perfect, *reviving the soul.*" It is "trustworthy, *making wise* the simple." It is "right, *giving joy* to the heart." And God's commands are "radiant, *giving light* to the eyes" (verses 7–8, emphases added). If something were available to you that revives you, gives you wisdom, brings joy to your heart, and brightens your eyes, all in one package or pill, wouldn't you want to get a hold of it and take it on a daily basis? We all need revival, wisdom, joy, and enlightenment. And God's Word contains all that…with the potential to work like a daily dose of vitamins for the mind, body, and soul.

Fresh Air from God

In 2 Timothy 3:16, we're told that all Scripture is "God-breathed." Think about that: Reading the Bible is like getting a breath of fresh air from the living God! It's like getting a second wind—from God—that teaches us, rebukes us, corrects us, and trains us in righteousness, so that we can be...drained? No, so that we can be "thoroughly equipped" for every good work. Now, *that* is fuel!

"Every part of Scripture is God-breathed and useful one way or another—showing us truth, exposing our rebellion, correcting our mistakes, training us to live God's way. Through the Word we are put together and shaped up for the tasks God has for us" (2 Timothy 3:16 MSG).

Did you catch that? Through God's Word we are *put together and shaped up* (in other words: fixed up, wound up, and restored) for the tasks God has for us.

That means getting your daily dosage of God's Word will help you handle the commotion of a busy house, tackle the endless trials of starting a new business, endure the stresses of deadlines on your job, face the frustrations of heavy traffic, stay cool during the frenzy of the carpool, or deal with the demands and disillusionments of ministry. In other words, God's Word doesn't just equip us to be informed theologians or Sunday school teachers. It gets us through everyday, ordinary life!

When I'm running on empty, I now ask myself how long it's been since I've refueled from the Word. And if it turns out I've been neglecting God's Word, I make it a priority to get back into feeding on the "green pastures" in the pages of His Word.

How God's Word Provides for Us

In Psalm 119, a long song that describes the Word of God in every stanza, we see many of the ways that Scripture keeps us from running on empty:

- It preserves us so we're not brought down by sin (verses 9,11)

- It enlightens us so we're not dragging (verse 18)
- It counsels us so we don't go the wrong way (verse 24)
- It strengthens us (verse 28)
- It liberates us so that we truly feel "free" (verses 32,45)
- It brings us delight (verses 35,111)
- It focuses us on what matters so we don't waste our time on worthless, idle pursuits (verse 37)
- It comforts us in our suffering or exhaustion (verses 50,52)
- It inspires us and gives us perspective (verse 54)
- It brings us wisdom, insight, and understanding (verses 98–100,130)
- It gives direction, so we don't get lost or confused (verse 105)
- It sustains us and prolongs our hope (verses 116,175)

One of the best pick-me-ups and leave-me-ups is reading and praying through the Psalms, a practice I mentioned in chapter 1. Another way to refuel from God's Word is to read it aloud. I've also found that when I'm longing for something more (which is another sign of running on empty), I need to ask what I've been filling myself with, because apparently it hasn't been satisfying. "My soul faints with longing for your salvation," says Psalm 119:81 "but I have put my hope in your word."

There it is! God's Word is enough. We can long for this or that, but His Word is the only thing that's going to be enough.

In 2 Timothy we're told that God's Word is profitable for teaching, for reproof, for correction, and for training in righteousness. It's also profitable for filling ourselves with the fuel and energy we need.

Getting into the Word

If you don't have a daily plan for refueling in God's Word, try any one—or eventually all—of these:

- Read through the book of Proverbs, and consider one proverb each day. For added benefit, summarize the proverb in a statement that will help to refuel you through the day.

- Read and pray through a psalm each day. Prayerfully rewrite it in your own words as a prayer to God. Fill up an entire journal this way.

- Do a word study that will refuel your soul. Take a word such as "strength" or "revive" and look up in your Bible's concordance the different verses in which that word appears. Read and write out each verse, and write anything else you learn about that word in the context of the verse.

- Read through one of the Gospels—Matthew, Mark, Luke, or John—and take note of what Jesus did to refuel, refresh, and keep going. Be sure to record your observations and thoughts.

Are you ready to try it? Get into God's Word and refuel, and see the difference it makes in your life. Jesus said: "Man does not live on bread alone, but on every word that comes from the mouth of God."[1] You and I both need His Word, which is a daily bread that helps to keep us spiritually healthy, keep us motivated, and keep us on a level path.

Pick-Me-Up Prayer

Living God, who breathed Your words of life into a Book, breathe Your life into my frail bones as I open Your Book and let You infuse Your life-giving words in me. Breathe Your wisdom into my mind, breathe Your gentleness into my heart, breathe Your likeness into my soul, and shine Your light into my eyes.

I want to be refueled by Your life-giving breath, Your life-giving words, Your life-giving ways.

Like Father, like daughter, I am made in Your likeness. So give me the likeness of Your strength, energy, and determination, starting with a desire to be in Your Word and refuel every day. On the days I need comfort, I know You will provide it most willingly. On the days I need strength, I know You'll give it bountifully. During times when I need wisdom, I know You'll provide it generously. And when I just need to hear Your voice, may it sound clearly in the depths of my heart. Thank You for Your promise to do "far more abundantly beyond all that we ask or think" (Ephesians 3:20 NASB). May I grab hold of Your abundant promises from Your precious Word. And may I then speak Your Word to others, sharing its life with them as well.

Don't allow me to long for anything other than Your life-giving Word.

I wait for the LORD, my soul waits,
and in his word I put my hope

(PSALM 130:5).

Chapter 3

Know Whom You're Trying to Please

I will listen to what God the LORD will say;
he promises peace to his people....
PSALM 85:8

I can't help but feel intimidated by the Proverbs 31 woman. She is revered as the godly woman and wife who has it all together. As I was reading the biblical definition of her one day, I tried to put her into today's context and culture. If she were around today, her description, based on verses 10–31, might read something like this:

> This is the ideal wife. Her husband adores her and so does everyone else in town. She waits on her husband hand and foot, and manages to have a life of her own as well. She does a lovely job decorating her home and always has

a refrigerator full of food when people drop by. She gets
up about 4:00 A.M. and cooks a low-cholesterol, highly
nutritious breakfast for her family, then goes about her
duties at home, work, *and* church throughout the day,
and then she stays up well past midnight, sewing clothes
(and making crafts) for everyone in her home. She has
a couple investments and side jobs in which she earns
money by day, then comes home and puts a gourmet
dinner on the table by night. She keeps an immaculate
house, runs an efficient ministry, keeps her husband
in fine standing in the community, and raises perfectly
behaved, unselfish, and hard-working children (who *don't*
need medication!). Her children wake up every morning,
calling her blessed, and her husband constantly sings her
praises. And, to sum up her life, she "smiles at the future"
or "laughs at the days to come."

Now do you see why I'm intimidated? Talk about running on empty!
Now if you and I did all of that day after day we would hardly be smiling
at our future…we wouldn't even want to get out of bed in the morning.
This woman's life seems insane! She never even sleeps…did you notice
that? She rises before the dawn (I'm thinking 4:00 A.M.) and her light
doesn't go out until way past midnight (that's got to be about 2:00 A.M.).
That means this woman does all this and operates on two lousy hours
of sleep! And it seems her life is going in a million directions. Every time
I look at this passage in the Bible I feel so guilty. I don't cook very well.
And I'm a spaz when it comes to sewing. And I make very little money
in my day job. And my child, who is now a teenager, does *not* rise up
every morning and call me "blessed."

There are some who say this woman is not real, but rather, she's
one writer's description of God's ideal woman. But real or not, if

her description is included in the inspired word of God as the "ideal woman," we have to sit up and take notice. There are reasons God wanted us to know about her. And I have a feeling one of those reasons involves verse 30: "A woman who fears the LORD is to be praised." This woman *fears* the Lord...not other people and what they're going to say about her. To *fear* the Lord is to have a wholesome dread of ever displeasing the Lord. It's having a love for Him that is so strong and so devoted that we fear disappointing Him. And in addition to fearing the Lord's disappointment in her, I truly believe this woman in Proverbs 31 is also a woman who *rests* in the Lord. Perhaps what God is saying to us in this description of the godly wife is that a woman who truly loves the Lord and abides in Him will be able to do all that she is called to do, because she knows intimately the One who can do all things through her. She won't necessarily be able to do all that *everyone else* calls her to do, but all that *God* calls her to do.

Answering the Call

Oh, if it were just that easy...to know exactly what God calls each of us to do. If you're like me, you've got several people calling you with things they'd like you to do. You may have a child calling you with something he or she needs. You might be at that stage of life in which your parents or in-laws are calling you and needing help. Now, how do we know which of those is the *Lord* calling us, as well? How do we discern *His* voice among the many cries for help in our day-to-day life?

> When we first do what He calls us to do, He takes care of the rest.

As women, we tend to be people-pleasers. We want to make everyone happy. We want everyone to get along. We want to accommodate, reciprocate, and generate harmony. That makes it easier for others' voices to sometimes appear louder than God's, and we can confuse His call with the calls of countless others.

The Proverbs 31 woman apparently heard God calling her to first take care of her home. She rose (while it was still dark) and probably was getting into God's Word and spending time with Him. She then made sure her family was well taken care of. Only after fulfilling these obligations did she venture out to take care of others. Above all, she knew *whom* she was trying to please. Not her husband, not her family, but God. And in doing so, the rest of the family was happy. (Remember that from chapter 1? Seek first God's kingdom and His righteousness, and all the rest will work out.)

Are there many people in your life whom you feel you have to please? Who is the *One* most important Person that you need to please? God Himself. We serve an audience of One. One God. One Master. One King. One Lord. And when we first do what He calls us to do, He takes care of the rest.

The days that I'm obedient to Him first are the days I get it right with my husband and my teenager and the rest of my world. Sometimes there are people in my life who don't understand why they got moved off my list of priorities that day. But I must ultimately answer to God, not them.

That's why I need to start my day with prayer, refuel with God's Word, and prioritize my relationships so I will do what is most necessary. When I realize that pleasing God first is most important, the guilt that comes from letting others down doesn't have the same hold over me.

When we know the one thing we must do (from the last chapter), we also know the One Person we must please. And that means there are days when our to-do list must be set aside, certain phone calls won't get returned, and some people won't get what they are asking us for...because we must respond to the One who will ultimately hold us accountable. Divine appointments will arise at times, causing us to set aside our work for the moment and deal with a situation that is more pressing. Divine interventions will occur at other times (that sometimes cause us to hold off from everything and just rest). If we can go through the day knowing we are pleasing the One to whom we will be held accountable, that will ease our stress and eliminate the burden of feeling we have to please everyone.

"Every day I let someone down," a friend of mine once told me, sadly. "I can't possibly be there for everyone. But I've had to choose carefully who I cannot afford to let down. And then I trust God that the rest of the people will understand."

Discerning God's Call

Do you know the One Person you need to please? Do you know what to do to please Him? As you rise early, spend that time in prayer, and spend it in His Word, you'll have a better idea of what is *really* expected of you from day to day...and what is able to fall by the wayside.

Jesus modeled that example for us. He often met with His heavenly Father and prayed, "Not My will, but Yours be done."

And at the end of His life here on this earth He prayed, "I have brought you glory on earth by completing the work you gave me to do" (John 17:4). Jesus could've spent most of His time healing the sick, raising the dead, feeding the multitudes of hungry people, and responding to every need that came His way. But instead, He paid close attention to all that His heavenly Father wanted Him to do, knowing His time on earth would be short.

We don't know how long our time on earth will be. But I believe every one of us wants to make the most of that time. To do that, we must not get sucked into the people-pleasing pattern of trying to do *all* things for all people. We must instead make sure we're pleasing the One who calls us to the few things He asks us to do.

And here's what is at the top of that list of few things:

- "Love the Lord your God with all your heart, and with all your soul and with all your mind" (Matthew 22:37). This is God calling you to prioritize your relationship with Him above anything else.

- "Love your neighbor as yourself" (Matthew 22:39). This involves loving and taking care of your family, treating others as you would yourself, and loving unbelievers enough to share with them the story of Jesus.

- "Whatever you do, work at it with all your heart, as working for the Lord, not for men" (Colossians 3:23). This involves your ministry. Whatever you do—teach, care for children, drive the carpool, cook, administrate, run a business, and so on—you are to do it *with a passion*. Obviously we can't do *everything* at peak levels of energy and motivation. So that means prioritizing some things over others, and even letting some things go.

- "Always be prepared to give an answer to everyone who asks you to give the reason for the hope that you have" (1 Peter 3:15). This means we need to be open to and prepared for the divine appointments God brings our way—those unexpected opportunities to share our faith and the gospel of Jesus.

Now there are other commands God gives to us in His Word, but if we're paying attention to those four, I believe we'll have them all covered. It may help to discern what *God* is calling you to do, as opposed to what your church, or your parents or your boss or your friends, or your own convictions are calling you to do, by asking yourself, What responsibilities can *only* be fulfilled by me?

- Only *you* can cultivate your personal relationship with the Living God.

- Only *you* can love your husband and take care of him physically, emotionally, sexually.

- Only *you* can parent your children. (No one else can take the place of Mom!)

- Only *you* can minister to others in the unique way that you do, whether it be writing, singing, teaching, caretaking, and so on. (For more on this concept see my book *When a Woman Discovers Her Dream: Finding God's Purpose for Your Life*, from Harvest House Publishers.)

I think you get the idea. There is only one of you. And there are millions of needs, causes, and jobs out there calling for your attention. There are demands on your schedule every time you turn around. Therefore you *must* know whom you are trying to please so you end up doing only those things He calls you to do. And if you're waiting for that relief that comes from being in a wide-open space…it happens when you get out from under the claustrophobic trappings of people's expectations.

There is energizing fuel in knowing you are pleasing the One for whom you were created. Keep your focus, my friend—and keep from running on empty—by knowing whom you're trying to please.

Pick-Me-Up Prayer

Lord, help me to see that You are the One I must ultimately answer to… and therefore, Your call on my life is most important. As David the psalmist once prayed: "Don't dump me, God; my God, don't stand me up. Hurry and help me; I want some wide-open space in my life!" (Psalm 38:21–22 MSG).

Life can crowd in around me when I'm trying to please everyone. Father, help me to see clearly Your agenda today, not mine. Bring to me those You want me to help, instead of having me rely on my own list of things to do. Help me see the priority in who needs help and what You—not others—expect of me. My prayer today is that by the time I lay my head down on my pillow at the end of the day, I will sense Your voice whispering, "Well done, my good and faithful servant. You have completed this day all that I have called you to do."

Chapter 4

Serve Out of Inspiration, Not Obligation

*I will praise you forever for what you have done;
in your name I will hope, for your name is good.
I will praise you in the presence of your saints.*

PSALM 52:9

During college I visited a friend from out-of-state during a spring break. That week, we became more than friends, and when I returned home, I discovered that his letters to me increased from one a month to one or two a week. In one of the letters, this marvelous man wrote: "I have many friends, whom I keep in touch with out of obligation. But I write to you, Cindi, out of inspiration." It was one of the most romantic comments anyone had ever said to me. And I never forgot it.

Since then, I have often put my relationship with God to the "inspiration test" and asked myself, How much of what I do for God is out of obligation, and how much is out of inspiration? I admit that sometimes, my rising early in the morning and spending time with Him and His Word is done because I know I *should* do it. Because of how it affects my day, there are times I do this because I *have* to. But wouldn't God much prefer me to be with Him and do things for Him simply because I *want* to? Simply because I'm inspired? Simply because I'm in love?

When I think of what I *have* to do, there is sometimes a sense of drudgery. But when I make a list of what I *hope* to do or *desire* to do, those things are much more exciting to look forward to.

Jesus several times pointed out the difference between serving Him out of law, and serving Him out of love. The religious leaders during His day were preoccupied with crossing every "t" and dotting every "i" when it came to fulfilling the exact letter of the law. But Jesus said that their hearts told the real story of their devotion and righteousness. They obeyed the law on the outside, out of legalism and obligation. But was there any love and inspiration in their hearts?

Finding the Inspiration

One of the things that makes me feel I'm running on empty is serving without a sense of purpose. Going through the motions. Doing the mundane, and wondering why I'm doing it. I often have to ask myself, Why am I doing this? Who am I doing this for? and, Is this really going to matter?

I used to get very frustrated cleaning the carpet stains at my church. A new building, with carpet that apparently wasn't "stain resistant," called for a lot of "spot cleaning" in the sanctuary and the adjoining long hallway every couple of weeks. Was I asked to do it? No. Did anyone expect me to do it? Of course not. But no one else was doing it. So I would grab the carpet cleaning solution out of the storage closet and get to it. There were times, on my hands and knees, with a bottle of carpet cleaner and an old dishrag in my hand, that I would think of the many other things I could be doing with my time that would be far more beneficial, in an eternal sense, for the church. *I'm a Bible teacher, not a carpet cleaner,* I would say to myself. *I'm the director of women's ministries, not the maintenance person!* Then one day I remembered a verse in Psalm 84 that I had recently taught on:

> I would rather be a doorkeeper in the house of my God
> than dwell in the tents of the wicked (verse 10).

I believe God paraphrased that verse for me, in that moment when I was on my hands and knees scrubbing the carpet, to read, "I would rather be a carpet cleaner in the house of my God than a big shot celebrity out there in the world." It was then that I realized that even the most menial, unglamorous, and unnoticeable jobs that are done for Him have eternal benefits if my heart is right. I also realized that God wanted to do some heart work on me during those moments—work that He couldn't do when I was up in front of the church wearing my "pastor's wife" hat or up in front of a class, teaching God's Word, or up on the platform at a women's event, speaking to hundreds. I now look back on that moment as one of the most precious lessons I ever learned from God. And it started with serving Him, I must admit, out of obligation…and the thought, *If I don't do this, no one will.*

If we start our work with a song, the inspiration will come.

Do I get inspired today to spot clean the carpet at church? No, of course not. But when I remember what He teaches me when I humble myself and do the job no one else wants to do, it gives me a little inspiration to get down there and learn what He has for me…and then pass it on. And what a love letter it would have been if I had said to Jesus, "There are many things I end up doing out of obligation, but what I do for you, Lord, (including cleaning this carpet) is out of inspiration."

Here are some ways to serve out of inspiration rather than obligation:

1. ***Whistle While You Work.*** I drew this idea from God's Word, not the seven dwarfs in *Snow White*. In 1 Thessalonians 5:17, we're told "give thanks in all circumstances, for this is God's will for you in Christ Jesus." When we thank God for a chore as we start to perform it, we are conditioning our minds to celebrate, not complain. Celebrate the fact that you are able-bodied enough to perform that task. Celebrate the fact that you even *have* a job. If it's your family's laundry you're setting out to do, praise God that you have a family to work for. If it's a big project that's closing in, be thankful you were entrusted with it. If we start our work with a song, the inspiration *will* come.

2. ***Look for the Lessons.*** Dare I say that some of my best speaking and writing material comes from doing the tasks no one else wants to do? Yet if we have the perspective that we'll learn and grow through taking care of a responsibility, we may approach the service with more of a willing heart.

3. ***Dedicate to Him the Task.*** Colossians 3:17 says, "Whatever you do, whether in word or deed, do it all in the name of the Lord Jesus, giving thanks to God the Father through him." Sometimes just saying, "This I do for You" as we start a task will keep us in perspective. At first we might say those words with a martyr complex, as if what we're doing is a huge sacrifice. But if we listen closely, we may hear Christ echoing our words from the cross:

"*This* I do for *you*." And that definitely puts into perspective every bit of work that we feel we're "suffering" through.

The next time you're facing a task, an obligation, a project, or maybe even a day or week that you're not looking forward to, go to the Lord first and pray, "Lord, make me willing to do this for You, and put a song in my heart as I do it."

When you bring such requests to God, He hears and He grants. In fact, His Word promises: "If we ask anything according to his will, he hears us. And if we know that he hears us—whatever we ask—we know that we have what we asked of him" (1 John 5:14–15).

Next time you're weighted down by obligation, ask God for the inspiration. And "how much more will your Father in heaven give good gifts to those who ask him!" (Matthew 7:11). The key to not feeling burned out, in a specific job or season of life, is to have the mind-set that what we are doing is for Him...and to restore the song in our heart.

Serving out of inspiration helps us to keep our focus.

Pick-Me-Up Prayer

Lord Jesus, You gave Your life for me. And yet all You ask in return is that I love You with all my heart, soul, and mind. Help me to remember that when the work seems to be a drudgery, when life gets hectic and I get tired, when I start to despair because of all that is expected of me. You were motivated by love for me in all that You did on the cross. Help me to be motivated by Your love for me—and what it cost You—in order to find joy in all that I set my hand to. So much of my attitude depends on where my focus is. I want to be focused on Your love and what You did for me, rather than on myself and how I feel. So from this day forward, grant me the grace to serve You with all my heart—not because I *have* to, but because I *long* to.

In the midst of my daily routine, may I remember Your words to me from Calvary: "*This* I do for *you*."

Chapter 5

Invest in What's Eternal

Store up for yourselves treasures in heaven,
where moth and rust do not destroy,
and where thieves do not break in and steal.
MATTHEW 6:20

I remember the day I was supposed to meet Alice for lunch. I didn't want to go. It had nothing to do with Alice. I just felt I was running on empty, and I didn't have much to give.

Alice didn't have a problem she wanted me to fix, or any type of issue she wanted me to help her with. She simply wanted to meet a friend for lunch. As we sat there and talked, I learned a lot about her that day. And I learned a lot about myself. We talked about raising daughters and how we each were raised. We expressed an appreciation for how God works in our lives. I shared with her some encouragement from Scripture and then prayed with her, asking God to give her wisdom and discernment as a parent. Then she prayed for me.

I left that lunch feeling grateful that I had met with Alice. I felt rejuvenated, refreshed, and refueled for the day. What had happened? God works in ways we sometimes don't anticipate. I've noticed that when I have little left to give but I show up anyway, God makes sure I'm blessed just for showing up. Sometimes God has a way of either filling me with the same energy I just infused into someone else, or He causes me to be encouraged by the person whom I thought I was going to encourage. I went to lunch that day expecting to pour myself into Alice, but she poured herself into me instead. Isn't it amazing how that happens?

> When you're running on empty, keep your focus on the fact that anything you do for Christ will last.

It must have something to do with the Golden Rule: "Do unto others as you would have them do unto you." The golden outcome of that, I believe, is that as we "do unto others" (in this case, provide encouragement, just as we'd want to be encouraged), God makes sure that encouragement comes back around to us. Sometimes God repays us through the kindness and encouragement of others. Whatever the case, I've found, most unexpectedly, that God often infuses energy into my life when I'm simply obedient and I do what I know He wants me to do.

Heavenly Banking

I suppose one analogy is that pouring yourself into another person is like putting something into a heavenly banking account. Imagine yourself making a deposit into an eternal bank account each time you lovingly pour yourself into someone else, each time you do something for the sake of being obedient to God or pleasing Him in some way. The "deposits" you make build up into a reserve you can dip into for energy—a reserve that provides generous returns while you're still here on earth.

Imagine getting a phone call from a friend in need. You look at your watch. You really need to stay home and finish up some work, rather than leave and help your friend. But this is a close friend, and you know she'd do the same for you. You also sense this may be a divine appointment through which God wants to work in and through you. So, perhaps with some reluctance, you go see your friend. While with her, you end up giving her biblical advice you needed to hear yourself. You end up encouraging her with some counsel you could use yourself. Afterward, as you drive away, you feel an extra amount of energy and fulfillment, knowing you had made yourself available to do something God wanted you to do. And the reluctance you once felt has turned into gratefulness. That's an example of how what goes around, comes around. What you put into another's life can come back and bless you before you even have a chance to think about what you've done. The heavenly bank account is already producing returns.

When you're running on empty, keep your focus on the fact that anything you do for Christ will last. Labors of love for Him or others. Taking the time to tell someone about Christ. Giving something up in order to give to another. And you will find that as you make deposits in that heavenly bank account, the returns will come back your way.

Jesus Experienced the Returns

In a sense, we see this principle played out in the life of Jesus. In John 4 we read that during a journey through Samaria, Jesus' disciples went into a town to get some food. Jesus, tired and thirsty, sat down by a well. A woman came and saw Him, and they started talking. Jesus then offered her living water. When the disciples returned, they urged Jesus to eat, and His response was, "I have food to eat that you know nothing about." His disciples were confused and thought that perhaps someone else had brought Jesus some food. Then Jesus said, "My food is to do the will of him who sent me and to finish his work" (verses 32,34).

Jesus arrived at Jacob's well tired, but after His encounter with the Samaritan woman, in which He offered her living water, and life and hope as well, He had been refueled. He was apparently energized by doing His Father's will.

Oh to be so in tune, so in sync with what God wants you to do that when it comes to ministering to others, His power fuels you!

Matthew 6:20 tells us to store up treasures in heaven (deposit into the eternal bank account that doesn't run dry), where moth and rust won't destroy it and where thieves won't break in and steal it. Although the intent of this verse is to warn us not to store up material possessions, I believe the principle works in relation to how we invest our time, as well. You see, when we are serving only ourselves, the moths of self-indulgence and the rust of self-absorption can make us feel worn out and empty. But when we invest in doing the work God would have us do, that accrues interest and produces a nice return.

Proverbs 11:25 says, "A generous man will prosper; he who refreshes others will himself be refreshed." In another translation, that verse reads "he who waters will himself be watered" (NASB). Go ahead—refresh others, and you'll be refreshed as well. And do it generously, and you may be surprised at the return!

Sowing Generously

The Bible says, "Remember this: Whoever sows sparingly will also reap sparingly, and whoever sows generously will also reap generously. Each man should give what he has decided in his heart to give, not reluctantly or under compulsion, for God loves a cheerful giver." And get this next verse: "God is able to make *all* grace *abound* to you so that in *all* things at *all* times, having *all* that you need you will *abound* in *every* good work" (2 Corinthians 9:6–8).

Did you catch that? Did you see how many times the words "all" and "abound" were used? That verse doesn't say "*some* grace will trickle down to you so that in a *few* things, every *once in awhile*, you'll have *a little* of what you need to get by in situations *now and then*."

To the contrary, that verse is packed full of "all" and includes "every" and twice mentions the word "abound." In another translation, verse 8 reads: "God will generously provide all you need. Then you will *always* have everything you need and *plenty* left over to share with others" (NLT).

Would you like to draw upon that supply so you'll have everything you need, and plenty left over to share with others?

Then invest liberally in giving of your time when it comes to following a directive from God. Store up the deposits in heaven. Remember: What goes around, comes around when you live in the realm of an all-knowing and all-loving God.

Pick-Me-Up Prayer

God, help me to sow generously when it comes to giving of my time to help another in need. Help me to remember my efforts are never wasted if I extend myself in love, take the call, go the extra mile, pick up the check, or pour myself out one more time. You invested your Son's life in me, Lord God, and for that I want to invest in You and those eternal rewards that await me. Give me discernment to know when the divine appointment is knocking at the door of my heart or the front door of my home. And give me the strength to respond, knowing You'll give me just what I need for as long as I need it.

When weariness encroaches upon me, and I'm feeling that I just can't give one ounce more, gently remind me that You gave Your all for me…and that I can give one more part of me to someone else, if done in Your name. And then grant me that peace and rest that You promise as I obey You.

Help me to remember this day that what goes around comes around in the name of Jesus, and that what I do for You will not go unnoticed in the heavenly realm.

Chapter 6

Act on Facts, Not Feelings

I have set the LORD always before me.
Because he is at my right hand, I will not be shaken.
PSALM 16:8

Let's face it: We are emotional beings. Some of us more than others. And we are too often influenced by how we feel. That can be dangerous at times.

Our feelings are unreliable because they change all the time. Our feelings are influenced by our circumstances, our moods, and our hormones. It could be quite a scary picture if we, as women, made major decisions in our life when we were at our emotional—or hormonal—worst. Yet that's what many of us do.

The psalm writers (literally, the "song writers") were very emotional as well. (Call them temperamental musicians, if you want!) They poured their hearts out in their songs, and if you read the Psalms as if they were song lyrics rather than verses or poetry, you will hear their hearts' cries and their emotions expressed in ways that sound like us today. And they lay out a "feelings to facts" response pattern in Scripture that we can learn from as well.

David's Emotional Response

In Psalm 4 David wrote,

> Answer me when I call to you,
>   O my righteous God.
> Give me relief from my distress;
>   be merciful to me and hear my prayer (verse 1).

Ever feel that way? Burned out, running on empty, needing relief and feeling like no one hears or cares?

Notice how David is completely focused on himself and how he feels. ("Answer *me* when *I* call…give *me* relief from *my* distress; be merciful to *me* and hear *my* prayer.")

In the next verse, David focused on what everyone else was doing to him. Then in verse 3, he shifted gears and reflected on some truths he *knew* about God: He knew "that the Lord has set apart the godly for himself; the Lord will hear when I call to him."

It's interesting that in the next two verses, David went on to list five actions he had to perform if he wanted the Lord to deliver him from his stressful situation:

—don't sin

—search your heart

—be silent (which means quit stressing)

—offer right sacrifices

—trust in the Lord

Then, in verses 7–8, after claiming his responsibility in calling to the Lord, David focused not on his feelings, but the facts—what he knew about God:

- He is the joy giver ("You have filled my heart with greater joy than when their grain and new wine abound.")
- He alone gives peace and rest ("I will lie down and sleep in peace...")
- He keeps us safe and secure (...for you alone, O Lord, make me dwell in safety.")

Did you notice the dramatic change in David over the course of the psalm? He went from, "Answer me when I call to you" and, "Give me relief in my distress" to, "You have filled my heart with greater joy" and, "I will lie down and sleep in peace."

David apparently worked through his feelings by focusing on the facts: "for You alone, O Lord, make me dwell in safety."

David Does It Again

In Psalm 6, again we find David emotionally down and physically spent. He is feeling discouraged, defeated, and overwhelmed because so many people are after him. Physically, he's wasting away. He's been running from his enemies for too long, and he's exhausted. Spiritually, he's dismayed and thinking God has forgotten him. Emotionally, he's depressed and feeling ready to give up. Talk about running on empty!

Listen to where he is, physically, and emotionally:

> Be merciful to me, Lord, for I am faint;
> O Lord, heal me, for my bones are in agony.

> My soul is in anguish.
>> How long, O Lord, how long?
> I am worn out from groaning..." (Psalm 6:2–3,6).

Do you ever feel that way? I do—when I'm overextended and I've pushed myself beyond the limits...when I'm feeling physically and emotionally run down.

At the beginning of Psalm 6, David is transparently sharing his feelings. But as in Psalm 4, in this song, David shifts from focusing on his *feelings* and instead, turns his attention to the *facts* to bring himself out of his depressed and rundown state. Look at what happened when he remembered the facts about God:

> Away from me, all you who do evil,
>> for the Lord has heard my weeping.
> The Lord has heard my cry for mercy;
>> The Lord accepts my prayer.
> All my enemies will be ashamed and dismayed;
>> They will turn back in sudden disgrace (verses 8–10).

What caused the dramatic shift in how David felt? He got his focus. It wasn't about how he was feeling. It was about the God who was going to take care of him. When he remembered the facts about God, his feelings waned and he got the energy and confidence he needed to get through his situation.

This is what David discovered by focusing on the facts about God, rather than his feelings:

- He may have *felt* like he was forgotten, but the *fact* is that God knew his case.

- He may have *felt* that God wasn't listening to Him, but the *fact* is that God in heaven heard his cry.

- He may have *felt* that God had rejected him, but the *fact* is that God had accepted—and acted upon—his prayer.

What About You?

You, my friend, may *feel* rundown and defeated, as if you can't do one more thing. But the *fact* is that you can do "everything through him who gives [you] strength" (Philippians 4:13).

You may *feel* you're up against a no-win situation, but the *fact* is that "with God all things are possible" (Matthew 19:26), and "everything is possible for him who believes" (Mark 9:23).

You may *feel* like you're at the end of your rope and you can't do one thing more, but the *fact* is that "those who wait for the LORD will gain new strength; they will mount up with wings like eagles, they will run and not get tired, they will walk and not become weary" (Isaiah 40:31 NASB). By waiting on God (which doesn't take a lot of energy, by the way), you'll gain new *strength* to *rise up, walk,* and even *run.*

The Pity-to-Praise Pattern

In Psalm 13, David repeats the pattern yet again. Only this time, he gives us a clear visual of what changed him from being on his face in pity to being on his feet in praise.

> How long, O LORD? Will you forget me forever?
>   How long will you hide your face from me?
> How long must I wrestle with my thoughts
>   and every day have sorrow in my heart?
> How long will my enemy triumph over me?
>   (verses 1–2).

Poor David—he really felt rejected and was pretty much flat on his face in self-pity. But look at what he says next:

Consider and answer me, O LORD, my God;
   enlighten my eyes, or I will sleep the sleep of death...
      (verse 3 NASB).

Now David is praying. He's gone from placing his face on the floor to kneeling in prayer.

I love how the song ends:

I trust in your unfailing love;
   my heart rejoices in your salvation.
I will sing to the LORD,
   for he has been good to me (verses 5–6).

Did you catch that? David, who earlier cried, "Will you forget me forever?" is now singing, "He has been good to me."

What took David from being on his face in pity to being on his feet in praise? Being on his knees in prayer. It was only by addressing God through prayer that David could get his focus off how he was feeling and remember two important facts: God can be trusted, and God is good. With that realization, David's stress in regard to dealing with his enemies rolled off his back and onto the capable shoulders of the Almighty God. And because of that, David was able to get up on his feet again! And he was no longer struggling with pity. He was now singing praise.

Bringing It Home

My prayers often start out in self-pity, too: "God, this isn't fair." "God, I just can't do all this." "God, I'm worn out and I need a break." But as I realize whom it is I'm addressing, I'm reminded of what He's capable of doing, and my pleas turn into praise as well: "God, I can't do this, but *You* can. You are all-capable. You put the sun and stars into place, and surely You can work out this situation, too. I realize that I am weak, and I know that You are strong."

When we get past our feelings and move on to the facts (of the situation and God), we gain a proper perspective. And, as an old hymn says, it's when we turn our eyes to the Lord that "the things of earth [that stress us out] will become dim compared to the light of His glory."[1]

I recently experienced a week during which I wanted to quit the ministry. (As a pastor's wife, I haven't quite figured out what that means, unless it's convincing my husband to leave his role as a pastor, which, unfortunately, many pastors' wives do, by the way.) My husband and I had met with a couple who recounted several ways that we had let them down over the past couple years. As I sat there, listening to how we had disappointed them and anticipating that they would leave the church for those same reasons, I was *feeling* frustration, pain, and anger. As I drove away from that appointment, I cried out to God and told him how I felt.

> When we bring our concerns to God we remember that He hears, and come to realize we're not alone in our struggles.

"God, I don't want to do this anymore," I screamed through tears, with all the car windows rolled up. "I don't want my husband to have to sit through another meeting in which someone tells him how he didn't meet their expectations. God, it hurts too much. I'm tired of pouring out and putting up because everyone just leaves in the end, anyway."

That's how I was feeling: Everyone eventually leaves. But in prayer, I was reminded of this fact: God will never leave me nor forsake me.

Instantly, God spoke to my heart: *Cindi, I went to the cross for you. And in light of what I did for you, do you know how many times you have*

disappointed Me? Do you realize how many times you have failed to meet
My expectations? And yet I have never left. And I never will.

In the quietness of that realization, in the moment my heart received
that truth, everything changed. I remembered whom I am serving and
to whom I will ultimately be held accountable. The reason I'm in ministry is not so I'll be appreciated or thanked or made to feel good. The
reason I do what I do is because of who He is. He is my Lover who will
never leave. He is my Savior and Redeemer. He is my Protector and Provider. And sometimes I have to come to the end of myself and be ready
to quit before I come back to the realization that it's all about Him, not
me. It's all about the facts (that He is God and worthy to be served) and
not my feelings (that it's hard sometimes and I just want to quit).

When we bring our concerns to God we remember that He hears,
and come to realize we're not alone in our struggles. We remember that
He gives strength, so we don't feel as if we have to give up. We remember
that He is able, so we don't feel as if we have to make things happen ourselves. We remember He is in control, so we don't feel as if we have to
do it all. We remember that we are but dust, and He is the wind beneath
our wings.

When our feelings lead us down a dark tunnel of despair, we must
switch on the light of what we *know* about God so we can find our way
back out.

Time to Get It Right

It's encouraging to see that in Psalm 34, David doesn't start his song
in pity as he did in Psalms 4, 6, and 13. Instead, he sings, "I will extol the
LORD at all times, his praise will always be on my lips." David finally got
it right! He learned to start off with the right focus, regardless of how he
was feeling. That is a choice, my friend. To whine or to worship. To be
absorbed in pity or to be emanating praise. We can be on our faces or
we can be up on our feet. I know which one I want. How about *you?*

Pick-Me-Up Prayer

I thank You and praise You, God, for the songs in Scripture that sound so much like they could've been written by me. How often I cry out to You about how I feel, absorbed in my own pity and problems. And then as my thoughts turn to You I'm reminded of the truth of who You are, and everything changes...my perspective, my mood, and my outlook on life. Thank You that You are not a God who shifts and changes along with my feelings. You are always the same, no matter how my moods change. You are always there, whether I feel like You are or not. You are always faithful, even when I am not. Thank You that You are the immovable rock of my salvation and my strong tower of refuge. Help me to set You ever before me and to remember that, because You are at my right hand, I will not be shaken (Psalm 16:8).

Chapter 7

Determine Whom You'll Trust

I will trust in you….in God I trust; I will not be afraid.
PSALM 56:4

I will take refuge in the shadow of your wings….
PSALM 57:1

I learned, in school, that self-confidence is good. I learned, through Scripture, that God-confidence is better.

I've found that the times I am most overwhelmed, stressed out, burned out, or simply feeling run down are the times when I have much to do and I feel I must do it all myself. I was recently on a book deadline (for this book, in fact), pulling details together for two consecutive out-of-state speaking weekends, wrestling with some decisions regarding my family's future, and trying to be available to a friend who needed help with the start-up of a business. I was feeling a bit run down. So when the cough developed and my voice started getting hoarse, I panicked.

I went to the doctor the first day I started feeling lousy and pleaded for him to put me on some sort of medication so I wouldn't lose my voice for the conference I was speaking at that weekend. I'd just returned from five speaking sessions at a conference in South Carolina, and I was headed to West Virginia to speak for another three sessions. "I *have* to have a voice this weekend," I told my doctor. (There was one time in my distant memory—I wish I could say it was just a nightmare—that I showed up at a speaking engagement with absolutely no voice! I didn't want *that* to ever happen again!)

The doctor prescribed a strong antibiotic and told me, on a Wednesday afternoon, that I'd be feeling 100 percent better by Monday. But I was supposed to speak on Saturday!

By the time I left San Diego Friday morning, I was dragging. The prescribed medication—and pain relievers—didn't seem to take effect. I was coughing badly, having difficulty swallowing, and was freaking out every time I opened my mouth and very little sound came out. My ears hurt, my throat hurt, even my teeth hurt! By the time I got to the little town of Clarksburg, West Virginia at midnight, I was a mess. Knowing I'd have to be up by 6:00 A.M. with a voice strong enough to speak for three hours that day, I started to cry.

"God, help me. I can't show up without a voice. Lord, they flew me all this way. These women will be there with great anticipation. God, I can't let them down. *Please* help me."

I remember...for several hours...falling off to sleep momentarily, then waking with the plea again: "God, *please* heal my throat and restore my voice."

I couldn't figure out why I seemed to be pleading, but getting nowhere.

Then I remembered. It wasn't about me.

Cindi, I'm the One who arranged for you to be here this weekend. Trust Me.

"But, Lord, I can't deliver a message You've put on my heart if I have no voice."

It's not up to you, Cindi. Trust Me.

"God, what do You mean it's not up to me? Am I supposed to hand someone else my notes and have *her* give the talks?"

Cindi, you are not in control. I AM.

Then I got it.

That control thing really stresses me out sometimes. It's probably what got me run down in the first place. I tend to believe it's all up to me. I've got to nurse myself back to health. I've got to get on that plane. I've got to have a strong voice. I can't let people down.

Humbled, I surrendered, there in my sleep, to the One who was in absolute control. "Ok, Lord, You are the only One who can make this work tomorrow. It's Your message, You will figure out a way for it to be delivered. They're Your women; You will figure out how to touch their hearts. All I can do is rest in You and trust You with tomorrow."

After whispering those words, I remember feeling as if I were being rocked to sleep in His arms.

The next morning, my voice was still scratchy and weak. My throat ached excessively unless I happened to have a cough drop in my mouth. The director of women's ministries at this wonderful little church had the women in attendance pray for me, and then I stepped up onto the stage and began. It was a bit of a rough start (coughing into the microphone isn't a pleasant audio experience for the audience). But the women were gracious. And the more I talked (here's the God-thing!), the stronger my voice became. I popped a new throat lozenge in my mouth each time I began another session, and God kept my voice intact long enough for the messages to be spoken. At the conclusion of my third talk, my throat burned, the coughing returned, and my voice was *completely* gone. But God came through! He gave me just what I needed at the time I needed it. I wasn't in control at all. And He wanted it that way.

Surrender the Control

Something happens to us when we realize we're not in control. It's called surrender. It's when we finally realize we really have no control over our circumstances. I admit I have a tendency to be driven, which puts undue stress and pressure on me. As a result, I end up feeling worn down, as if I were running on empty. When I back off and verbally acknowledge that God is in control and not me, then I feel an actual release of mental, emotional, and spiritual stress. It's as if my mind, soul, and spirit were finally relaxing so they can function the way they're supposed to.

> God's ways are always higher than ours.

When you and I become stressed out, it's often because we're thinking of all that we have to do. When we feel defeated, it's because we're not hoping and trusting in what God can do. The question, then, is this: What am I believing about God that isn't true? In my situation in West Virginia, I was asking God to "help me" instead of saying, "Take over...I'm done." I was believing God would come to my assistance once I asked and told Him how, rather than giving up altogether and saying, "I need *You* to take control of this situation....*You* let me know what You want me to do."

God's Promise

Scripture says God is able to do "immeasurably more" than we could ask or imagine (Ephesians 3:20). In The Message, that verse reads: "God can do anything, you know—far more than you could ever imagine or guess or request in your wildest dreams!"

That's a pretty strong statement, isn't it? *Immeasurably more* than we can even imagine…that's a big God! That's a capable God. And that makes our problems, and the things that drain us, small in comparison.

All through the night before I spoke to the women in West Virginia, I fretted over what it would be like to open my mouth and not be able to speak the next morning. I wasn't imagining that God would come through in such a way that women would be blessed and I would learn a huge lesson in the process. I was only thinking of my remedy. God's ways are always higher than ours (Isaiah 55:9)!

Ironically, while I was at the conference, the words to one of my sister's songs, *You Alone* (which I had the director of women play between the sessions), were ringing out to me after each speaking session, and served as God's gentle reminder to me of who had it all in control:

> You are the One
>   who loved me from the start.
> You gave me breath
>   and formed my beating heart.
> It was You who put the meaning
>   deep in my soul.
> You are the One
>   who never leaves my side.
> You're always there
>   no matter where I hide.
> It was You who gave me comfort
>   during the storm.

You alone are worthy
of my praise.
You alone are Lord
over all my days.
All I am, I willingly give;
in You, alone, will I live.

You are the One
who never lets me go.
You sent your Son
to die so I would know.
It was You who knew I needed
your endless grace.

You alone are worthy
of my praise.
You alone are Lord
over all my days.
All I am, I willingly give;
in You, alone, will I live.
In You, alone...will I live. [1]

What area of control do *you* need to surrender to God so that He can bring relief and refreshment to your life? In what ways do *you* need to acknowledge that He's in complete control, so you can finally say, "In You alone will I live"?

My friend, you can place your confidence in yourself and run yourself ragged trying to do it all. You can place your confidence in someone else, and eventually be disappointed and let down.

Or...

- You can trust the One who created you and has your days

numbered and has ordained each one of them, according to His will.

- You can trust the One who has walked through tomorrow and next week and next year and knows what's on the horizon and what's on your heart.

- You can trust in the only One who can rock you to sleep once you surrender it all to Him in the wee hours of the morning.

Now, who will *you* trust so that you're no longer running on empty?

Giving-It-Up Prayer

You, Lord, are the One who controls all things—my schedule, my time, my circumstances, my life. Help me to recognize that truth each day by taking to You all that wears me down and stresses me out and leaving it in Your capable hands. To rest is to trust. Therefore I rest in You and Your ability to do all things through me…or without me at all. Forgive me for the times I have thought it's all about me. Remind me, instead, that it's all about what You want to teach me, how You want to strengthen me, and ways You want to mold me to become more like Christ.

This day, when I start to feel worn out, remind me that You are the wind beneath my wings and that I can soar in Your strength. And when I start to get frustrated at not being in control of things, do what it takes to get the point across that I need to get off the throne of my life again and let *You* be God.

In You, alone, will I trust.

Part II:
Keeping Fit

…let us strip off every weight that slows us down.…
And let us run with endurance the race that God has
set before us.

HEBREWS 12:1 NLT

We can feel run down in a number of ways, not just mentally through the wrong focus, but physically through the wrong input. Keeping a clean heart, a positive attitude, a healthy diet, our body moving, and ourselves in good company will produce energy in our lives. In order to run without tiring, we must first lose the weight that slows us down and then fuel up on what will keep us going. It's all a matter of keeping fit…

Chapter 8

Keep a Clean Heart

I will praise you with an upright heart...
PSALM 119:7

I will be careful to lead a blameless life...
PSALM 101:2

I remember a time in my life when I was unusually listless. I had little
motivation to get anything done. I slept a lot. I often stared blankly out
the window when I should've been getting something done. I avoided
being around people who would inquire as to what was wrong. And I
remember thinking, *Why do I feel like I'm running on empty?*

Looking back now, it was also a time when I was harboring sin in
my life. I was in rebellion concerning an issue God wanted me to deal
with. I was compromising in an area where I knew God's standards were
clear. I was holding onto something and not wanting to surrender it to
God. I felt heavyhearted. The dichotomy was tiring. The deception was

> Sometimes our energy is sapped because our heart simply isn't right.

draining. The sin was entangling me. And I was feeling the weight of it. It wasn't until I poured it all out to God, and surrendered the sin, that I felt the burden lifted and my energy renewed.

When our hearts aren't right, we will feel down and empty. Bitterness, unforgiveness, unconfessed sin, dishonesty, or simply an ungrateful heart or bad attitude can drag us down.

The writer of Hebrews wrote this at the beginning of chapter 12:

> ...let us strip off every weight that slows us down, especially the sin that so easily hinders our progress. And let us run with endurance the race that God has set before us. We do this by keeping our eyes on Jesus, on whom our faith depends from start to finish (verses 1–2 NLT).

Have you ever considered that you might feel physically run down because there's sin in your life? Have you ever thought about what might be the "sin that so easily hinders" your progress?

The Wear and Tear of Sin

King David, in Psalm 32, pondered the impact of sin and wrote this song in response. Listen to his lament before he confessed the sin in his life:

> When I refused to confess my sin, I was weak and miserable, and I groaned all day long [sound familiar?]. Day and night your hand of discipline was heavy on me. My strength evaporated like water in the summer heat (verses 3–4 NLT).

Sometimes when we're worn out it's because we're simply doing too much. But sometimes our energy is sapped because our heart simply isn't right.

"Above all else, guard your heart," says Proverbs 4:23, "for it is the wellspring of life." Another translation says: "Watch over your heart with all diligence, for from it flow the springs of life" (NASB). When we feel dry and empty, it could be because the "wellspring of life" (our motivation, our energy, our liveliness) is stopped up. So how do we guard our heart and keep it clean so our "springs of life" don't dry up?

- *Lay it all out* before God. He already knows what you are struggling with. Laying it all out is your way of surrendering it to Him and saying, "I want a fresh start."

- *List the things in your life that you need to give up* to keep your wellspring flowing. Sometimes when we put our problem in writing, we are able to see, in black and white, what it is we need to release to God.

- *Look to God* to put a fresh perspective and healthy motivation back into your life. Wait upon Him with great anticipation that He will give you the desires of your heart, which includes a desire to please and not grieve Him (Psalm 37:4).

Look what happened to David when he laid his problem out before God:

> Finally, I confessed all my sins to you and stopped trying to hide them. I said to myself, "I will confess my rebellion to the Lord." And you forgave me! All my guilt is gone. (Psalm 32:5 NLT).

In fact, David wrote Psalm 32 in retrospect. From a fresh heart made right, he said,

What joy for those whose rebellion is forgiven, whose sin is put out of sight! Yes what joy for those whose record the LORD has cleared of sin, whose lives are lived in complete honesty! (verses 1–2 NLT).

Did you notice the spring in David's step as he sang that song? That spring came after he got his heart right—after the "wellspring" of his life was restored.

Do you need to regain that spring in your step? Do you need to get those "springs of life" flowing out of you again? Then it may be time for a heart-check. Here is a sampling of the kinds of problems that can hinder or entangle us. You might be able to think of others as well:

- Rebellion to something God is asking of you.
- A habit or lifestyle that you know is not pleasing to God.
- Refusing to give God, financially, what is rightfully His.
- Unforgiveness toward another person.
- Bitterness toward God, or someone else.

Now, confess each sin that is entangling you. To confess means to agree with God that what you are doing—or not doing—is wrong. Ask Him to deliver you from the weight that these sins entail and give you the strength to turn your back on them once and for all. And when your heart is made right, you will be able to say with David, "You are my hiding place; you protect me from trouble. You surround me with songs of deliverance" (verse 7).

Listen to Your Songs of Deliverance

If you're feeling dragged down by a heart that isn't right, run to your "hiding place" and confess what's on your heart. And listen for the "songs of deliverance" that surround you:

♪ "If we confess our sins, he is faithful and just and will forgive us our sins and purify us from all unrighteousness" (1 John 1:9).

♪ "Turn, O LORD, and deliver me; save me because of your unfailing love" (Psalm 6:4).

♪ "In the day of my trouble I will call to you, for you will answer me" (Psalm 86:7).

♪ "Create in me a pure heart, O God, and renew a steadfast spirit within me....Restore to me the joy of your salvation and grant me a willing spirit, to sustain me" (Psalm 51:10,12).

Listen to those songs in another translation...it's like hearing your favorite lyrics sung to a different tune:

♪ "...if we admit our sins—make a clean breast of them—he won't let us down; he'll be true to himself. He'll forgive our sins and purge us of all wrongdoing" (1 John 1:9 MSG).

♪ "Return, O LORD, and rescue me. Save me because of your unfailing love" (Psalm 6:4 NLT).

♪ "Pay attention, GOD, to my prayer; bend down and listen to my cry for help. Every time I'm in trouble I call on you, confident that you'll answer" (Psalm 86:6–7 MSG).

♪ "God, make a fresh start in me, shape a Genesis week from the chaos of my life....Bring me back from gray exile, put a fresh wind in my sails!" (Psalm 51:10,12 MSG).

Those are your songs of deliverance. A Deliverer stands by, ready to hear your confession, accept your acknowledgment of sin, grant pardon, and release those springs of life again. In Acts 3:19 we're told, "Repent, then, and turn to God, so that your sins may be wiped out, that *times of refreshing* may come from the Lord." "Times of refreshing"... doesn't that sound appealing?

I love how David ends Psalm 32: "So rejoice in the LORD and be glad, all you who obey him! Shout for joy, all you whose hearts are pure!" (verse 11). Do you want the energy and motivation to "shout for joy"? You'll have it when you daily bring your heart to God and let Him give you a clean bill of health.

The first step in keeping fit, then, is to keep a clean heart.

Clean-Me-Up Prayer

Lord, if my rundown feeling is from the weight of sin on my shoulders—sin that I haven't surrendered to You—then reveal that to me so that I can give it all to You. How long, Lord, can I linger in sin when Your unfailing love keeps penetrating my heart, longing to set me free? Show me where I need to be cleaned up and deliver me from the weight and burden of that sin. Release me to run again, straight to Your arms for my forgiveness and freedom.

I long to have a pure heart and clean hands before You. As the psalmist sang, "Soak me in your laundry and I'll come out clean, scrub me and I'll have a snow-white life. Tune me in to foot-tapping songs, set these once-broken bones to dancing. Don't look too close for blemishes, give me a clean bill of health….Going through the motions doesn't please you, a flawless performance is nothing to you. I learned God-worship when my pride was shattered" (Psalm 51:7–9,16–17 MSG).

Thank You that I can rejoice with songs of deliverance when I acknowledge my sin to You. And thank You for Your promise to restore my joy. "Oh give me back my joy again; you have broken me—now let me rejoice" (Psalm 51:8 NLT).

Chapter 9

Keep Good Company

My eyes will be on the faithful in the land, that they may dwell with me;
he whose walk is blameless will minister to me.

PSALM 101:6

"Bad company corrupts good morals," says the Bible.[1] Bad company also runs you down.

On the other hand, "as iron sharpens iron, so one man [or woman] sharpens another."[2]

Just as bad company can run you down, good company can get you going. So, the people whom we choose to hang out with can make all the difference in the world when it comes to being drained or being energized.

Studies show that when we are around positive people, we become more positive ourselves. And positive people—those who see the glass as half full rather than half empty—are by and large healthier than negative people.

I've learned, through years of ministry, that there are two kinds of people: the builders and the drainers. The positive people and the negative people. In other words, those who fill your tank and those who drain you. Those who fill you are the people who build you up, challenge you, inspire you, stretch you, encourage you to see the good side of things, and generally help you to become a better person. We all need people like that in our lives to help keep us growing, keep us accountable, and keep us from becoming a critical or negative person.

My friend Chris is the "older" woman in my life (but not by much... most people think we're the same age!). She challenges me to grow spiritually and lovingly warns me if she thinks I'm making poor choices with my priorities or running myself ragged with my schedule. She's also someone I can laugh, shop, and relax with.

Then there's Diane, the "younger" woman in my life (by about 15 years...I *wish* people thought we were the same age!). Her energy and vivaciousness is contagious. Her teachable spirit is encouraging. When I pour myself into her, I end up rejuvenated. When I hear her laugh, I laugh, too. I never leave from a conversation with Diane feeling weighted down or drained. That's because she's a positive person—and because of that, it's healthy for me to be around her.

Every Tuesday, I have breakfast with Diane and lunch with Chris. Just like a healthy meal or a dose of vitamins, they are regulars in my life who help keep me positive, keep me growing, and keep me accountable.

Then there are the drainers. You know who they are. I simply mention the word, and their faces come to mind. They always need something. They're always down on something. They're always telling you their troubles. And every time you're with them, after awhile you're thinking, *I'm not sure how much longer I can endure with this person.* In the overall scope of things, you give and they take. And it's rarely the other way around. Truth is, you can't afford to be around someone like that…especially if you're prone to running on empty.

Keeping It Positive

How can you deal with the negative influences in your life? Here are some simple ways to keep life more positive:

Limit your relationships to builders, not drainers—It's always good to have an abundance of builders and preferably *no* drainers. But that would happen only in a perfect world, right? In reality, there are drainers everywhere, and we cannot always avoid them. Perhaps you have a family member or coworker who is a drainer. If so, then do your best to limit their influence on you. Being positive is a choice, and when it comes to drainers, you may have to make careful and conscientious choices in terms of limiting your interaction with them.

> If we've got a God who can work all things for good, certainly we can please Him by looking for the good in all things.

Look for the good in every situation—One positive element of being around a drainer is that you learn what you'll sound like if you become one of them. For me, it's seeing firsthand what I don't want to be. If it turns out you've got to be around a drainer, look for the good in the situation to balance out the bad.

Let it go—One of my friends constantly tells me, "You'll get over it." Sometimes, however, he gives more of an order: "Get over it." Most of the time when this happens, he's responding to my complaints, or what he calls "bellyaching." (And most of the time, hearing him say, "Get over it" when I wanted sympathy just makes me mad!) But once I *do* get over it, I find I have more energy, which I'm able to use toward getting something done rather than pouting, whining, or bellyaching.

Do you have a friend or mentor who can tell you to "get over it" when you start to complain or dwell on the negative? You need that person in your life to help you let go of the things that pull you down.

The Right Perspective

So what do you think? Can you identify the positive people in your life and keep them around you? Can you approach life today, positively, by seeing the glass as half full rather than half empty? One way to do that is to take Romans 8:28 to heart: "We know that in all things God works for the good of those who love him, who have been called according to his purpose." If we've got a God who can work all things for good, certainly we can please Him by looking for the good in all things.

Keep fit—body, mind, and soul—by keeping good company and keeping it positive.

Pick-Me-Up Prayer

Thank You, Lord, for Your gift of friendship and for the positive people You've placed in my life. Help me to discern, in the friends You've given me, who are the builders and who are the drainers, and how to spend my time accordingly. Give me the strength to pour myself into those who have so faithfully poured themselves into me. Show me those influences in my life that are contributing to a critical spirit and that weigh me down. And turn my eyes toward those who emanate a joy and energy that obviously comes from You.

Lord, may I not only find and be around positive people, but may I become such a person myself so that others may be lifted up and encouraged. May I see the good in all things, be thankful in all things, and cultivate a heart of praise to get me through the day. And with Your strength and Your Spirit fueling me, may I be a magnet of motivation and energy to everyone who comes in contact with me today.

Chapter 10

Keep a Healthy Diet

We are the temple of the Living God.
2 CORINTHIANS 6:16

I must admit, a few of my close friends laughed or rolled their eyes when they heard I was working on *this* chapter. Mainly because I've been known to overindulge in chocolate (or anything sweet for that matter), I tend to drink too much soda, and I would live on fast food if I could get away with it. It's common knowledge that I attend Jazzercise® classes simply so I can eat whatever I want. But I've also noticed that what I eat directly affects my moods and my energy level, and whether or not I feel like I'm running on empty.

Our eating habits are usually shaped by how we were raised and fed. Within me is a strange dichotomy. My father was a health food nut (we weren't even allowed to have white bread or white sugar in the house when I was growing up). My mom, on the other hand, was the Junk Food Queen. (She had a secret stash of sweets. Up until about a year ago, she had a cupboard full of chocolate in her kitchen...seriously! The entire cupboard was full of chocolate cookies, Pop-Tarts®, candy, cereal...everything that has chocolate in it. Suffice that to say, I tend to take after my Mom when it comes to sudden sweet cravings. But closely connected to that is the conviction (from my father's influence) to eat healthy and smart.

Both my parents, who are now in their sixties, seem to be living the results of their food choices. Dad is healthy as ever, even though he eats too much butter (real butter) and lives on meat and potatoes (but has hereditarily low cholesterol, of course). My Mom, however, was recently diagnosed with adult onset diabetes (goodbye, chocolate cupboard) and has suffered from increasing health problems over the past few years. As a child, when it came to food, I witnessed two extremes in my parents. And now as an adult, I must determine the right balance between the two.

Eat for Your Energy Level

According to Pamela M. Smith, author of *Eat Well, Live Well* (Creation House, 1992), every person can control their energy level, health, and well-being by deliberately choosing to eat foods known to have positive health effects. So we don't have to follow the patterns we saw from our parents and say, "I don't know any better." There are so many resources available today that we can't help but be informed and know better what's good for us and what isn't. And when it comes to running on empty, we can choose foods that will help boost our energy and make us feel so much better.

"Good nutrition is never more important than when we're stressed," Smith says. "But good eating usually goes out the window in times of stress—just when we need it most as our defensive shield."[1]

Smith adds, "When stressed, the body goes into a conservation mechanism to allow optimum defense. In this state of conservation, 1) the body's metabolism slows, storing excess energy for a fight or flight response to stress; 2) the body's blood sugar fluctuates, stimulating an appetite for higher-calorie foods to provide the needed energy; and 3) the body will retain excess fluids to keep the body in proper hydration for the defense."[2]

That metabolic slowdown explains the physical side effect of quick weight gain during stressful times. Overeating due to stress also plays a part, but when we're under stress, "the body does a lot more damage with what comes in," Smith says. That's why nutrition is so important when you're stressed or running on empty. As our blood sugars fluctuate, our energy drops, our mood drops, and our appetite soars. That's why you and I tend to crave chocolate (which is known to be mood-inducing) or other sweets when we're stressed or feel as if we have no energy.

Since our bodies can act weird when we feel stressed, here are some practical (and sane!) suggestions to keep in mind when it comes to food choices when you feel you're running on empty. (And just in case you're worried, these tips are not my own common sense regarding eating, but suggestions that have their origin in *Prevention Magazine*. These tips are designed to help women find more energy through what they eat and drink.)[3]

Begin with a bowl of bran—Eating a morning meal rich in fiber can make you more alert during the day. A study at Cardiff University in Wales found that people who ate cereal with 6 to 12 grams of fiber in the mornings showed a 10 percent reduction in fatigue. They also had fewer memory problems, fell asleep at night faster, and were less depressed. The reason? Fiber may lead to the release of fatty acids that create energy. It also helps alleviate constipation, and studies have found that people who switch to high-fiber diets are more energetic, possibly because they feel lighter and more comfortable.

Pack a power lunch with peanut butter and bananas—Lunch should leave you feeling energetic, not sleepy. Large meals loaded with empty carbohydrates are sure to sap your energy. A quick and inexpensive solution is to have the same lunch you would feed your child. (Children are loaded with energy, right? Maybe that's because they're eating better than we are!) The "feed yourself what you feed your child" approach works only if you make peanut butter and banana sandwiches for your child. Bananas are packed with potassium, a mineral your body needs in order to convert the sugar in your blood into energy.[4] Peanut butter is high in magnesium, which gives your cells much-needed energy. Spread all those nutrients between two slices of fiber-rich whole wheat bread, and you'll get enough energy to fuel your afternoon. (And if you're concerned about peanut butter because of the "fat" and calories it contains, stay tuned for the next chapter: As long as you "keep moving," you can eat all the peanut butter you want!)

Drink water before *you're thirsty*—If you're feeling tired or have a headache by midday, it could be a sign of dehydration, a sign that you're not getting enough water. I know that six to eight glasses of water a day seems unreasonable, but if you drink a glass of water before and after every meal, that's six glasses already. (Drinking water before a meal also curbs your appetite, helping you to eat less.) And if you're feeling thirsty at any time, it means you've already reached some level of dehydration. So take sips of water each time you pass a drinking fountain, whether you're thirsty or not. My husband, Hugh, also taught me that I'll get more than my daily allotment of water (and save money, too) if I order water with my eat-out meals rather than soda pop. And refills of water are much better for your body than refills of soda.

Brew a mug of green tea—I know, green tea might not have the best taste, but it's good for you. Green tea is a much better pick-me-up than coffee or latte. Although it does have some energizing caffeine, it also contains theanine, a compound that has a stress-reducing effect on your brain. There are now green tea powders in flavors such as peach and lemon that actually taste good, too. One scoop in a a glass of water in the morning serves not only as a sweet treat, but as a way to start your day with energy, as well as pack your body with immunity-producing antioxidants. (And if you can't part with your morning coffee, consider trading your large mug or thermos for a small one. Large doses of caffeine can cause the jitters, insomnia, and anxiety. Instead, drink half a cup in the morning and half in the afternoon, or a quarter of a cup every hour, for a more gradual intake of caffeine.)

Avoid an excess of sweets—(Okay, this suggestion is mine.) Although sweets tend to perk you up and give you a sugar high, they also have a down side—literally, the sugar low, which can make you feel lower than you did before you indulged. Sweets also tend to bring on headaches and increase migraines in some people. You can still have fun food (I sure will!), but you may want to consider sweets to be a once-in-awhile reward rather than an everyday staple.

> You *can* live a new legacy when it comes to eating healthy and keeping a good diet.

Keep It Natural

Remember, your body is the temple of God. Is that temple filled with healthy, energy-producing food or with empty calories, junk food, and strange-sounding additives you can't pronounce?

When it comes to making diet choices, I try (and I stress the word *try*, for the most part) to go with what's more natural. The baked potato over the french fries. The sugar over the sweetener or sugar substitute. The egg over the cholesterol substitute. The milk over the soda. And the whole wheat bread over the Pop-Tart®! That advice came from my paternal grandparents (wonderful old Swedes who lived on a farm, lived on health food, and lived into their mid-nineties, by the way). The diet strategies I got from my mother's side of the family, however, included unusual ideas such as the banana diet (eating only bananas for a week to lose weight), the tomato soup diet (eating only tomato soup for four days), the grapefruit diet (eating only grapefruit to lose weight), and the chocolate shake diet (you get the idea…). Any diet that has you eating only bananas (or some other particular food) and cutting out certain essentials needed by your body will merely be a quick attempt at losing weight that will mess up your body's metabolism and do more damage to your health in the long run.

When it comes to dietary and eating habits, do your research, use your common sense, and eat the foods that will produce energy and keep you from feeling run down. And if you have baggage in the dieting or eating department, realize that, in Christ, you are a "new creation" (2 Corinthians 5:17). As such, you have within you the resources to live in a more disciplined manner. You *can* live a new legacy when it comes to eating healthy and keeping a good diet.

Pick-Me-Up Prayer

Lord, I praise You that I am fearfully and wonderfully made. You've given me a body so complex, so intricately put together, and You want me to take care of it.

Thank You for giving me such liberty when it comes to what I can eat. And yet Your Word says I should do everything in moderation. Give me the self-control to "buffet my body and make it my slave" when it comes to choosing what to eat and how much. May food not control me, but may I control it. Help me to be grateful each time I bring something to my lips, and mindful that I should be careful to fill my body with that which is pleasing to You. Help me to fill this temple of Yours with energy-producing fuel rather than empty calories and artificial chemicals that make me feel sluggish and slow.

Above all else, may I develop responsible eating habits, with an eye toward being healthy. Help me to take good care of my body. Thank You again that I am fearfully and wonderfully made.

Chapter 11

Keep Moving

I discipline my body like an athlete, training it to do what it should.
1 Corinthians 9:27 nlt

I praise you because I am fearfully and wonderfully made;
your works are wonderful, I know that full well.
Psalm 139:14

Believe it or not, one of the best ways to keep from running on empty is to keep yourself moving.

To the contrary, we tend to think the more we slow down and the more we sleep, the more energized we'll feel. But, don't buy the lie.

Being sedentary makes us more sedate. Sleeping longer makes us more sluggish. On the other hand, the more we move, the more we'll be able to. The more energy we expend, the more we'll have later.

"I wish I had that kind of energy," a young mom used to tell me—

years ago—every time I passed by her house with my one-year-old daughter in a stroller or in a baby seat on the back of my bicycle.

A new mom at 39, Nona was wiped out, physically, by noon every day, doing all she could to keep up with a toddler.

I wish I had known then what I know now about exercise. And that's that the energy you wish you had to exercise will be there once you *start* to exercise.

Most of us don't feel energized by the thought of keeping ourselves moving. I don't get a sudden burst of energy every afternoon before my Jazzercise® class. There are days I almost literally drag myself there, thinking I'd rather sit at home and read a book than jump around and lift a few weights for an hour. But once I'm there—and I see all my friends, and Holly, our energetic instructor, gets us going—then the adrenaline kicks in. I've got the energy. And the next day, it's much easier to go back.

Benefits of Exercise

Studies show that the more you exercise, the more you raise your metabolism and resting heart rate. This means your body will continue to work even after you've stopped. That's why people who exercise on a regular basis lose weight, have more energy, and look and feel more energetic.

Most people today are not as active as they should be. Thirty-five percent of adults don't exercise at all. And more than 60 percent of adults do not achieve the recommended amount of regular physical activity. More than half of the adults in the United States are estimated to be overweight or obese, and according to the U.S. Surgeon General, recent national increases in obesity have more to do with lifestyle than genetic makeup. The U.S. Surgeon General now reports that a failure to exercise at least three times a week for a duration of at least 30 minutes each time is equivalent to smoking a pack of cigarettes a day!

If that isn't enough motivation to get me moving, I don't know what is! With that statistic in mind, not only is it healthy for us to exercise, it's extremely unhealthy for us *not* to. So exercise is no longer optional; it's a necessity of life! I feel at my worst when I haven't exercised in awhile. If I miss a few workouts, it not only shows, but I can feel it as well. I tend to get depressed, feel sluggish, and, well, gain weight.

> Find a friend and set some personal exercise goals together.

Plan the Exercise into Your Day

Because regular exercise is just as important as eating and sleeping regularly, you must have a plan to make it happen. It needs to be written into your day or scheduled, like a do-or-die appointment. (In reality, because of its importance to your health, exercise may very well be a do-or-die scenario.) Here are some ways to prioritize exercise so you'll keep moving:

- Join a health club and then visit it regularly. Make sure you join one that has an array of options:
  — Several pieces of cardiovascular equipment (such as stationary bikes or treadmills)—if there are too few, you may get discouraged about having to wait to get on a bike or treadmill, and then you'll quit going

  —aerobics, kickboxing, step, or stretch classes

  —free weights or machines to help you firm and tone

  — a swimming pool (but only if you'll use it)

  — certified personal trainers to help you establish and

maintain an exercise routine that works for you and keeps you motivated to continue

- If you're not into the health club scene or can't afford it, invest in some aerobics videos and work through a few of them a week. (A favorite one of mine is *Bodies in Motion with Gilad*. It includes a stretch section, an aerobic section, and floor work to firm and tone the body parts every woman needs to work on.) Make sure you have someone hold you accountable for playing that video a few times a week and working out with it!

- Find a local park or trail where you can walk. When the weather's bad, walk through an indoor mall. Just don't get distracted and become tempted to shop!

- Take a swing dance class or other type of class that will get you moving. My friend has a daughter in Irish dance. After about a year, she found herself in an Irish dance class made up of other moms of Irish dancers. She now has fun while she works up a sweat.

- Find a friend and set some personal exercise goals together. Join a class or club together. Plan to walk a few times a week with each other. Hold each other accountable and reward each other for your successes. Try to outdo each other with extra exercise slipped in during the week. As the Bible says, "Two are better than one, because they have a good return for their work: If one falls down, his friend can help him up. But pity the man who has no one to help him up!" (Ecclesiastes 4:9–10). I can't stress the importance of having accountability when it comes to exercise. (Even with me, I know if I skip a few Jazzercise® classes, I'll hear it from Holly and the rest of the girls!) Find that friend (or friends) to keep you moving and hold onto her (or them)!

In addition to a regular exercise plan (moving at least 30 minutes in duration for a minimum of three days a week—remember that Surgeon's General report!), we need to see exercise as a way of life and take the "keep moving" option over the sedentary one every time we have the choice. That way, we train ourselves to always be exercising without even thinking about it. Here are some ways to intentionally add even more exercise into your day so it becomes a lifestyle:

- Park farther away from your grocery or department store so you have to walk a little further to get to the store. Those additional steps will do you good. (Don't let me find you waiting near the front of the store until the first or second parking place next to the entrance becomes available!)

- Take stairs rather than elevators or escalators. A good climb is good for your heart rate, as well as for the back of your hips and thighs.

- If it's within reasonable walking distance, and it's not raining, snowing, or hailing, just walk. (As a rule, don't take the car if you're going less than a mile. I mean, really.)

- Do some stretches at your desk at work. Sitting up in a straight-back chair, stretch your legs out in front of you and flex your heels so your toes are straight up. (Pull in your stomach and put your shoulders back as you do this, too.) Then point your toes forward and repeat this motion 10 times. The more you intentionally and carefully stretch throughout the day, the less prone you are to injury.

- Run when you get the chance. I often find myself in a hurry and, if I've got comfortable shoes on, I'll take the opportunity to run, or at least jog, to wherever I need to go. The temporary rise in your heartbeat will be good for you. And regardless of what you look like while running, you'll look better in the long run for doing it.

- Keep a lookout for creative ways to keep moving. Do you have a bicycle you haven't touched in years? If so, grab a helmet and take the bicycle for a spin. Is your local health club advertising a one-week free pass? Try it out and see if it works for you. Do your friends have a trampoline? Try it out the next time you're at their house.

Find Ways to Keep Moving

That last suggestion is one I've done myself. I know a family that has a *huge* trampoline in their backyard. Each time I'm at their house, I have to get a few jumps in. Tina, the mother of the family, laughs at me: "There goes Ms. Cindi on the trampoline again," she tells her kids. And they all run out to join me. And keeping up with kids on a trampoline will keep you moving, burn some calories, *and* be a lot of fun—all at the same time! Common sense would say that a 40-year-old woman should not be doing split-jumps and attempting aerial flips on a trampoline. But really, we're as young as we feel, right? And as long as we *can* move, we should. Chances are, the more we move now, the more we'll be able to later. For safety's sake, just make sure you don't fall *off* the trampoline. (That might get you in a condition where you *can't* move for several months.) Fortunately for me, my friends have a safety net around their trampoline, which eliminates that danger.

Make it a point today to look for an opportunity to keep moving, whether by using a trampoline, a stationary bike, or stairs. And you'll find yourself feeling much better, and healthier.

Pick-Me-Up Prayer

Thank You, my Creator and loving heavenly Father, that I am fearfully and wonderfully made. I was wrought with skill—knit together in my mother's womb and hidden to the rest of the world, but fully known by You.

Help me to see exercise as a key part of getting my body, Your temple, into tip-top shape for You. If I am able to skip and jump for joy, I can praise You. If I am able to carry another's groceries, as well as carry their burdens in prayer, I am serving You. Remind me of the many ways I can glorify You if I keep my body in shape.

Deafen my ears to the enemy's taunts that I will never look or feel as good as I want to. Silence my own negative voices that tear myself down and ultimately criticize You for how You have put me together.

May my song be as David's: "I praise You because I am fearfully and wonderfully made; your works are wonderful, I know that full well" (Psalm 139:14).

Chapter 12

Keep Your Sleep

I will lie down and sleep in peace,
for you alone, O LORD, make me dwell in safety.
PSALM 4:8

A friend of mine recently started a new business. After a few months of working long hours and seeing few results, he became discouraged. He felt overwhelmed by all there was to do and became worried about advertising his business effectively and attracting enough customers to make his venture successful.

One evening, as he drove home discouraged, his business partner called to tell him that the new sign that went up on their building was lit and shining brightly. It happened to be the biggest and brightest sign in the entire shopping center, and was clearly visible from the freeway offramp.

"It's advertising brightly even as we speak," my friend told me later that evening from his home, sounding more encouraged.

"And it will be advertising brightly even as you sleep," I responded, reminding him of God's promise in Psalm 127. God actually says in that psalm that we are wasting our time getting up before the crack of dawn and going to sleep past midnight, toiling and striving to make things happen, because the God of the universe "gives to His beloved even in his sleep" (NASB).

When we do what we can and honor God with it, God has a way of honoring us in return. And one of the ways He does that is to give to us, even in our sleep. What a peaceful, relaxing truth to know, especially when we feel we're running on empty at the end of the day. God will take what I have done and bless it even while I sleep.

> There's nothing better to do as you fall asleep than to commune with your heavenly Father.

Yes, God wants us to be productive and to have a good work ethic. He tells us in His Word that we are not to get lazy to the point that we sleep too much and don't put in a good day's work (Proverbs 6:9–11). But there is only so much time in a day that you can work, and then you need to sleep. Most people need six to eight hours of sleep per night to function properly. God designed our bodies to need rest.

Listen to what God's Word says in Psalm 127:1–2 about our tendency to overwork and neglect sleep:

> Unless the LORD builds the house [or the business, or the home, or the project], they labor in vain who build it; unless the LORD guards the city [or whatever it is you're concerned about], the watchman keeps awake in vain. It is vain for you to rise up early, to retire late, to eat the bread of painful labors; for He gives to His beloved even in his sleep (NASB).

So the next time you have work piled up and you think you need to stay up late to "work through" or "worry through" it all, remember that God has a way of "working it out" if you just rest in Him—literally. God commands us to rest, and when you walk away from your work and determine to get some rest in order to keep your body healthy and refreshed, you are being obedient—and God blesses obedience.

Tips for Better Sleep

If you have trouble falling asleep at night, try one or more of the following suggestions, which are designed to help you trust in God, rest in Him, and reap His blessings as you sleep:

- Pray nightly before going to sleep. By giving your cares and concerns to God, you are getting them off your mind and putting them in God's hands. In 1 Peter 5:7, we're told to "cast all your anxiety on him." Does praying before going to bed help you sleep? Absolutely. (How many times have *you* nodded off to sleep during prayer?) There is a sense of relief that comes from handing your cares over to God. And if you fall asleep in the middle of your prayers, don't feel guilty for "falling asleep on God." Be thankful instead that He rocked you to sleep in His arms. There's nothing better to do as you fall asleep than to commune with your heavenly Father.

- Avoid rigorous exercise in the evening hours. It gets your heart rate going, gives you more energy, and may make it more difficult for you to shut down your body and fall asleep.

- Avoid caffeine after 4:00 P.M., especially if you regularly have difficulty falling asleep.

- Avoid decongestants or other medications that may make it

difficult for you to fall asleep. (Any non-drowsy medicine may lead to insomnia.)

- If you're finding it difficult to get the wheels of your mind to slow down, try getting up and writing down your thoughts, writing out your to-do list, or writing out anything that keeps rolling around in your mind and is keeping you from falling asleep. Then return to bed with an "empty" head. ☺

- Try reading before bed. It will make your eyes tired and help induce sleep.

- Counting sheep has never worked for me, and besides, what's the point? But I have found it sleep-inducing to imagine heaven. Closing your eyes and letting the Lord transport you to a peaceful, relaxing place where you have no worries and absolute joy is a great relaxation exercise.

- Stretch regularly and you'll sleep better. You can quiet your mind, release muscle tension, and beat anxiety with a few stretches a day. In a study done at the Fred Hutchinson Cancer Research Center in Seattle, 86 women who were having trouble sleeping needed 60 percent less sleep medication and had 30 percent less difficulty falling asleep when they stretched four times a week.[1]

Making Sleep a Priority

So what do you think? Can you make sleep a high-enough priority so you're not running on empty? Sleep helps you refuel and re-energize for another day. Like exercise, it's not optional. Rather, it's a necessity if we want our minds and bodies to function properly.

Pick-Me-Up
(or Put-Me-to-Bed) Prayer

Lord, thank You for the gift of sleep. You gave me so many hours in a day to work, and then You graciously provided the nighttime so I could rest my mind and body. As I obey Your command to rest, thank You that You honor me by blessing me, even in my sleep. When I lay my head down tonight, help me to trust in Your provision and rest in Your love.

Thank You, too, for Your sweet words in Scripture that tell me I can sleep at peace, knowing You are the One watching over me:

> I sleep and wake up refreshed because You, LORD, protect me
> (Psalm 3:5 CEV).

Thank You, God, that after a rough and trying day, You not only rock me to sleep in Your arms, but You watch over me lovingly as I sleep.

Chapter 13

Keep at It

*Let us not become weary in doing good, for at the proper time
we will reap a harvest if we do not give up.*
GALATIANS 6:9

*Not that I have already obtained all this,
or have already been made perfect, but I press on...*
PHILIPPIANS 3:12

If ever there was a time when I wanted to quit, it was after the Spring
Fling. I had just organized, spoken at, and hosted two tables of friends
for my church's biggest women's event of the year. Although it went
over as a success, my assistant and I were the first ones to see and hear
about what didn't go well (those behind-the-scenes details that no one
else knows about). We were both exhausted, physically and emotionally.
We looked at each other later that night, as the other women were still

rejoicing in the wonderful evening they'd had, and we both said quietly, "We're never going to do this again."

Have you ever felt ready to quit right after a great victory? Call it post-performance blues, or the big letdown after the big production, but the feeling of wanting to give it all up after giving your all is a very real problem. It's after you've poured yourself out completely that you find yourself running on empty, and find it difficult to muster any strength to do anything more.

And those are the times when we most need to keep at it.

Wanting to Quit

We see many examples in the Bible of people who gave their all and then wanted to give it all up. For example, there's Elijah, an Old Testament prophet. He climbed to the top of a mountain, took on the false religious system of his day, called down fire from heaven, and proved there was a God in Israel. Then he singlehandedly killed 450 false prophets who worshiped the false god known as Baal.

> Jesus kept at it, even though there were many times He could've given up.

But after a huge day of spiritual victory, Elijah got the bad reviews (namely a threat from the evil Queen Jezebel, who wanted him dead), and he sunk to an all-time low. He ended up running down that mountain in fear, running 16 miles in the rain, and finding himself in a low spot in the desert. He not only wanted to quit the ministry, but to quit life altogether. He actually pleaded with God to take his life. God saw that His servant was tired and needed some comfort and consolation and confidence to help get him up on his feet again.[1]

Another example is King David, who saw many great victories as a warrior and king. But on the heels of his victories, he, too, often felt like giving up. His ability to keep at it—in his relationship with God and in his daily duties—revolved around choosing to praise God in spite of everything.

Our Primary Example

Jesus is our foremost example of One who kept at it, even though there were many times He could've given up. Jesus dealt daily with 12 men who never seemed to get it. He gave to His disciples example after example of what it meant to live by faith, perform miracles by faith, and believe in God for the impossible, but they still couldn't get it right.

Listen to Jesus' words of frustration when He must have felt like giving up on His disciples:

- When the disciples were freaking out in a storm—even though Jesus was right there in the boat with them—He asked, "Why are you so afraid? Do you still have no faith?" (Mark 4:40).

- After Jesus miraculously fed the 5,000, walked on water, and then fed another 4,000, He rebuked His disciples, saying, "Why are you talking about having no bread? Do you still not see or understand? Are your hearts hardened? Do you have eyes but fail to see, and ears but fail to hear? And don't you remember? When I broke the five loaves for the five thousand, how many basketfuls of pieces did you pick up?…And when I broke the seven loaves for the four thousand, how many basketfuls of pieces did you pick up?…Do you still not understand?" (Mark 8:17–21).

- When a man complained to Jesus that the disciples could not drive out the evil spirit from his demon-possessed son, Jesus replied, "O unbelieving generation…how long shall I stay with you? How long shall I put up with you?" (Mark 9:19).

Yet Jesus did not give up on the Twelve. He kept at it, shaping them and molding them and instilling in them what they would need so they could eventually turn "the world upside down" (Acts 17:6 KJV).

We are encouraged, in Scripture, not to give up, but to keep our eyes on Jesus, "the author and perfecter of our faith, who for the joy set before him endured the cross…" (Hebrews 12:2).

What was the joy that was set before Jesus on His way to the cross?

- The joy of knowing He was obeying His Beloved Father. ("…not my will, but yours be done"—Luke 22:42.)

- The joy of His eternal reward. ("Therefore God exalted him to the highest place and gave him the name that is above every name, that at the name of Jesus every knee should bow, in heaven and on earth and under the earth, and every tongue confess that Jesus Christ is Lord…"—Philippians 2:9–11.)

What is the joy that is set before *you* as your motivation to keep at it when you feel like quitting?

- *The Joy of Knowing Christ.* "I want to know Christ and the power of his resurrection and the fellowship of sharing in his sufferings, becoming like him in his death, and so, somehow, to attain to the resurrection from the dead" (Philippians 3:10–11). Just to know that whenever we keep at it we are getting a glimpse of what it's like to be Jesus should cause our hearts to fill with joy. That is God's will for us: to become more like Christ in every way.

- *The Joy of Pressing on for Christ.* "I press on to take hold of that for which Christ Jesus took hold of me" (Philippians 3:12). In other words, if Christ kept at it on His way to the cross so He could pay the penalty for my sin, surely I can keep at it (with a joyful heart) in the tasks ahead of me, which are nothing compared to what Jesus endured for me on the cross.

- *The Joy of Pleasing Christ.* "I press on toward the goal to win the prize for which God has called me heavenward in Christ Jesus" (Philippians 3:14). I know God will reward me for my faithfulness in doing not only what I *feel* like doing, but what I know *needs* to be done.

- *The Joy of Maturity.* I am becoming more mature by keeping at it even when I feel like quitting. After all those "keep-at-it" verses we just read from Philippians 3, verse 15 tells us, "All of us who are mature should take such a view of things." Anyone can quit when the going gets tough. It takes the truly tough and mature to keep at it.

It is when you are making that final push to keep at it that you will be able to feel God provide a lift underneath your wings and help you to soar and go the distance. After the Spring Fling that I mentioned earlier, even though my assistant and I were so drained that we felt like quitting, we pressed on. We took the entire summer off from any event planning. We called it our "Summer with the Savior" (instead of our "Summer with Stress") and let Him refuel us through His Word. We realized we needed to turn our eyes to Jesus and what He has for us (rather than on the work ahead) and the opportunity to become more like Him, no matter what that entailed.

Can you go that extra mile, my friend, when you feel like stopping dead in your tracks? Can you continue the race a little longer, taking it in small strides instead of trying to sprint through it all? Can you cut your project into bite-sized pieces instead of trying to swallow the whole enchilada? Can you go far enough to complete only what it is you must do today? Of course you can...because the One who can do all things through you is standing by, ready to help you:

- "I can do everything through him who gives me strength" (Philippians 4:13).
- "Embrace this God-life. Really embrace it, and nothing will be too much for you" (Mark 11:22 MSG).

When it comes to keeping fit, keep at it. When it comes to walking the straight and narrow, keep at it. When it comes to eating right, keeping your body moving, and making sure you're getting enough sleep, keep at it. And you'll find motivation in knowing you are not alone. The Lord is right beside you, helping you to *keep at it*.

Pick-Me-Up Prayer

Thank You, Jesus, that You, more than any other, know what it's like to want to quit. You even prayed, "Father, if you are willing, take this cup from me; yet not my will, but yours be done" (Luke 22:42). While on this earth, You had your share of frustrations, and You lived with impending death. Yet You pressed on for the joy set before You. Certainly Your example of keeping at it can help me to do the same in my life. Just as Your love for me kept You on the course of the cross, may my love for You keep me on the course You have set before me. For all the times I've been frustrated—about life, about work, about church, about ministry—help me to see Your face at the end of the race. And with You in mind as my prize, may I run joyfully toward the finish line.

For You, and You alone, Lord Jesus, I will forever keep at it.

Part III:
Keeping Fresh

Open my eyes that I may see wonderful things in your law.

PSALM 119:18

Keeping our minds focused and our bodies fit is not enough. We must keep our souls fresh…full of praise, full of anticipation, full of wonder. God has given us a sense of awe, an ability to enjoy, and a thirst for adventure. But we can so easily miss these if we're too busy running here and there and not noticing what is all around us. Once we find our hideaway, learn to sing in all things, simplify our lives, take time to play, and explore the wonder and beauty of God's creation, we can keep our lives energized and our souls refreshed.

It all comes together by keeping fresh…

Chapter 14

Find Your Hideaway

I will say of the LORD, "He is my refuge and my fortress..."
PSALM 91:2

You're my cave to hide in, my cliff to climb.
PSALM 31:2 MSG

My friend was at her wit's end. She was tired from working long hours, frustrated at not feeling heard, and overwhelmed by all there was to do with three children, a stressed-out husband, a large house, a dog, a fish, and some lizards.

When I called, she was nearly at her breaking point. She vented. I listened. We both cried. We talked about how sometimes it's just life. Sometimes it's just that we need to get away from it all. I asked if she had somewhere—anywhere—to go in that house where she could be quiet and alone and we could pray.

"Go to your bedroom closet and shut the door," I instructed just as her husband was coming home to help control the kids and the chaos.

115

She took the phone with her upstairs and into her large walk-in closet and shut the door. She sat on the floor, and we prayed. There, in the dark and quiet of her bedroom closet, my precious overwhelmed friend found her hideaway with God.

It's when we find our hideaway with God that we can begin to hear His sweet songs of deliverance. "You are my hiding place," sang David in Psalm 32:7, "you will protect me from trouble and surround me with songs of deliverance."

Could it be that as we hide away in God, and find that place where we can be alone with Him, that we begin to sense His protection and experience the comfort of His deliverance?

Psalm 32:7 in The Message reads like this: "GOD's my island hideaway; keeps danger far from the shore, throws garlands of hosannas around my neck."

> It's when we find our hideaway with God that we can begin to hear His sweet songs of deliverance.

When I imagine God as my "island hideaway," I realize I can go away with Him in my heart at any time, anywhere, and find that place of rest and worship. But sometimes it's not so easy when we have distractions all around us and noise coming from every direction. That's why it's important to *find* our hideaway and retreat there often. For most of us that means "creating" our hideaway—finding a place and making it our sanctuary where we can go to get away from it all, get quiet, and get refueled.

Where's Your Hideaway?

Maybe your hideaway is your back patio in the early morning. Maybe it's your study, with a fire going and a cup of hot cocoa on your desk. Maybe you're like my friend and your hideaway is your bedroom closet. Or maybe you have to resort to the quiet of your car during your lunch break at work. Wherever that place is, it must be readily available and a place that you condition your heart and mind to respond to once you get there.

"I have a chair in the corner of my house," one woman told me, "and as soon as I sit down in it, my mind and heart know what I'm there for. I can close my eyes, release my thoughts, and focus on God pouring rest into my life." *That's* what I mean by conditioning your heart and mind to respond once you get there.

I grew up in a small two-bedroom house with five people—my parents, myself, my brother, and my sister. When my second brother was about to be born, making us a family of six, we added on to our house. We tore down the wall in a closet and attached a long hallway that led to two large bedrooms, a utility room, an office, and another bathroom. But the first door you came to in that long hallway was what we called "The Quiet Room." My mom had insisted we have a little room built, no larger than a closet, that could serve as a "sanctuary" in the house. There was just enough room for a desk, chair, and a lamp. In this hideaway, she wrote music, read her Bible, and prayed. It was *the room* (with a lock on the door) where anyone could go to shut out the world and pray. We didn't use that room at all as kids. (Since when do children need to get away from it all and have some silence? That's what they get for punishment, not a reward!) But three months before I got married, I moved back home (and by that time, only Dad was living in the house), and the little room became *my* sanctuary. It was where I spent the first hour of my day—alone with God, reading His Word, pouring my heart out to Him in prayer, and listening to Him in the quiet of the morning. I look back on those "retreats" as precious times with my Lord. How I long for a "Quiet Room" today!

God says our bodies are His temple. That means there's a sanctuary—a "Quiet Room"—in our hearts where we can hide away with Him every day. But to help us get there, we need a physical "Quiet Room" or a resting place or a hideaway where we can be alone.

If you don't yet have a hideaway—a place to go to be alone with God where no one else can bother you—then you *must* find one. If you have a house full of people who often need you, tell them clearly that when Mom is in a certain room, or a certain chair or a certain closet, it means she mustn't be disturbed. Train your loved ones that when you're in that place, you're away with God, and when you come back out, they'll be glad you took the time to calm down and refuel. Hopefully they'll be able to see the difference in you! Remember, when Moses had been with God on a mountain for 40 days, his face shone, and everyone knew he had been with God (Exodus 34:29–35). When you emerge from your hideaway, everyone should know that you, too, have been with God.

Ideas for Your Hideaway

Here are some possible hideaway ideas, if you have yet to find yours:

- A quiet room, such as a sewing room or study, where you can close the door. (Make sure it's a room that's tidy, so you won't be distracted by all the work you have to do once you get there.)

- A favorite chair in a quiet corner of the house. (This may depend on *when* you go there, whether or not it's your sanctuary. In that case, time your "hideaway with God" when the area around the chair is most quiet and accessible.)

- A place outside that feels peaceful. (For example, a backyard pond or pool, a deck in the evening, a place along your morning walking route where you can sit in peace and quiet.)

- A place where you can pull it all together or pour it all out. (Get creative! This may be your bathtub, your coat closet, your basement, or a cleaned-up corner of your attic.)

Once you find your hideaway, go there often to rest, refuel, and rejuvenate. It's a necessity, not a luxury, if you want to keep from running on empty.

Pick-Me-Up Prayer

Lord, I long for You to pick me up and hide me away with You. Show me where that place is—where we can get together alone and You can quiet me with Your love. The day can get so hectic and the noise so loud that I need to just get away and hear the sound of silence. You command me in Your Word to rest...show me how I can rest at Your feet in some way, every day. Draw me to that special sanctuary where You can pour rest into my life. I long to be there, just as You long to meet me there. May my hideaway be one of our favorite places to commune together. "How lovely is your dwelling place, O Lord Almighty!" (Psalm 84:1). And wonder of wonders, Your dwelling place is within me. Whether I'm in that physical sanctuary or not, may I find a way to hide away with you in my heart every day.

Chapter 15

In All Things Sing

I will sing of your strength,
in the morning I will sing of your love...
PSALM 59:16

I grew up in a musical family. Seems like we were always singing. It started out with me, my sister, and my mom singing for church groups, community clubs, and so on. Eventually, my sister and mom moved on, musically, without me. When my daughter, Dana, was born, my husband and I became a singing family. My husband would sing songs to Dana to get her to eat or fall asleep. I remember singing to her in the car as she drifted off to sleep, and singing to her around the house. Now Dana sings in the shower, sings herself to sleep, and sings in a ministry group that performs at local churches.

Singing, for Dana, has become a way of life. And my hope and prayer is that perpetual praise to God will become a way of life for her, as well. As she learns to sing even under stress, she will be able to turn pressure into praise and let it go.

Singing brings a smile to our faces, and we tend to sing when we're happy. Singing can also help pick us up when we feel stressed or when we're running on empty. That's because singing is biblical. That's right—singing is one of the most reiterated commands in the Bible. Throughout the Psalms we're told to sing:

- "Sing to the LORD, you saints of his…" (Psalm 30:4)
- "Sing praises to God, sing praises…" (Psalm 47:6)
- "…come before Him with joyful songs" (Psalm 100:2)
- "Sing and make music in your heart to the Lord…" (Ephesians 5:19)

God knew that singing would have a way of helping to lift our hearts, lighten our load, and put the things of life in perspective. In fact, He told us to sing in *all* circumstances so that we might overflow with praise rather than crumble under pressure.

> When we sing, we are obediently telling God that no matter what this day holds, we are choosing to praise Him.

In All Things Sing

In 1 Thessalonians 5:18 we're told, "In everything give thanks; for this is God's will for you in Christ Jesus" (NASB). In other words, "In all things, sing."

When I was hurt by a situation in ministry recently, I played a CD and sang a song about how God carries me. While I was on my way to an appointment I was dreading because I figured it would be another situation in ministry which wouldn't go well, I began to sing, "I love You, Lord" and realized that the situation I was about to enter was a "sacrifice of praise." Though I didn't look forward to the appointment, I headed into it with a heart of obedience. (In all things, sing.) Once when I was frustrated with my husband (about something that was really my fault, I'm sure!), I started to sing, and that reminded me of who was in control.

How does singing help energize you when you're running on empty?

- Singing lifts your spirits.
- Singing exercises your vocal chords, and thereby helps you with your breathing.
- Singing is a form of expression, and expressing your feelings is healthier than keeping them bottled up inside.
- Singing is a form of praise, which helps put all of life in the right perspective.

The Results of Singing

When we sing throughout the day, we become less focused on our troubles. When we sing, we lift up others as well. And when we sing, we are obediently telling God that no matter what this day holds, we are choosing to praise Him. When we sing in our suffering (or stress), praise Him in our pain, and lift up our voices under the weight of our burdens, we are obediently offering to God a sacrifice of praise that puts us in perspective and lightens our load. Remember the last part of 1 Thessalonians 5:18: "Give thanks in all circumstances [in all things sing], *for this is God's will for you* in Christ Jesus." It couldn't be said any plainer. God's will is that we learn to sing in everything...the good, the bad, the mundane, the marvelous. By singing in everything, we are acknowledging who is in control and living accordingly. We're keeping a spring in our step and a song in our hearts because we are at peace, not drowning under the pressure.

How much lighter our day would be if we lived by the motto, "I will sing to the Lord all my life; I will sing praise to my God as long as I live" (Psalm 104:33)!

Keep yourself fresh by keeping a song in your heart. In all things, sing.

Pick-Me-Up Prayer

"My heart is steadfast, O God, my heart is steadfast; I will sing and make music" (Psalm 57:7). How much lighter my days would be if I held onto a song, rather than stress. How much freer I would feel if I were to make music, rather than haste. Lord, slow me down long enough to enjoy a song, and help me to find the right perspective in the middle of it. How often You have brought calm into the chaos of my day by putting a song in my heart and having me sing it. Bring to my mind the words and to my heart the melody so that I can live lighter and freer and with a song in my heart.

And may Your Word continually inspire me to sing so I can say, as the psalmist did, "Your decrees are the theme of my song wherever I lodge" (Psalm 119:54).

Chapter 16

Simplify the Day

When I awake, I will be satisfied with seeing your likeness.
PSALM 17:15

We are complicated creatures. Some of us even specialize in taking the simple and making it strenuous. In our fast-paced world full of countless options every time you turn around, sometimes just the decision-making process becomes a task.

When I walk into Starbucks with my husband, I'm amazed at how complicated it can be for him—or anyone else, for that matter—to simply order a cup of coffee. Tall (which really means "small"), Grande (a classy word for "medium") or Venti (which really means "tall")? Fat or nonfat? Caffeinated or decaffeinated? Whipped cream or no-whip? And then…is it latte, mocha, cappuccino, or frappucino? Whatever happened to the 49-cent cup of coffee my Dad used to order at Denny's? We live in a world of multiple options and countless choices, which can, at times, drag us down and tire us out mentally.

Believe me, I can start to feel weary just looking in my closet every morning and trying to decide what to wear. It's not that the choices are limited and so it's a tough decision. The problem is that there are *too many* choices. My closet, like the rest of this world, has gotten complicated. There's just so much to choose from. So for me, the first chore in the morning is when I'm made aware that I need to eliminate the choices and simplify the day.

Whether it's the length of your to-do list, the number of clothes in your closet, or the amount of papers on your desk, less is more when it comes to handling the stress. The longer the list, the messier the closet or room, or the higher the pile, the more stressed we become just by looking at it. That's when simplifying becomes a must. Downsizing the mess and clearing the clutter are just a couple ways you can simplify the day so you feel less stressed and have more breathing room.

Creating Space

Clear the Clutter—It's amazing what a lift you can get just by clearing off your desk. I know one man who would, every once in a while, simply brush everything off the top of his desk and into a box. The box then went into a cupboard or somewhere out of sight. Now, that's scary to me. Because at least some of those papers that just got shoved into a box might need some kind of response, and I'd be stressed over what didn't get done. But if you're the kind of person who has useless papers on your desk that you've pored over countless times and shuffled even more times but have still gotten nowhere with it, maybe it *is* time to get out a box and, in one fell swoop, clean off your desk.

Toss the Trash—I'm a keeper. I have to force myself to toss things—such as papers with information written on them that I'm sure I'll need someday. Old magazines with articles I may want to refer back to someday. Clothes in my closet I haven't worn in years, but keep just in case they come back into fashion one day. Enough is enough! I have to force myself to go with the motto "If you haven't touched it, worn it or even looked at it in a year, let it go." Once I finally get rid of things, I rarely want them back….or even remember that they're gone. So if you have things that are doing nothing more than simply taking up space, let them go.

Limit the List—Every morning I write a to-do list (sometimes I write it the night before). I tend to include on that list *everything* that, ideally, I'd like to get done that day. Is my list realistic? Not often. But I know that if I shoot high, I will probably get more accomplished. Unfortunately there are days when the first couple items on the list take so long to accomplish that they never get crossed off. And that makes me feel like I didn't get much work done. I've learned lately to limit my lists by focusing on the top three priorities of the day. There are also times when I add tasks that don't take much time to do because they will give me a greater sense of accomplishment at the end of the day because I was able to cross them off. Perhaps it's all mental, but I find it easier and more fulfilling to accomplish a few things than to never finish many things.

> The more content I am with just having Jesus, the simpler my day is.

Create Some Open Space—We all need open space in our life. Like margins that help keep a comfortable distance between the words on a page and the edges of that page, we need margins of open space on the edges of our lives. You can create that margin, or open space, by simply planning it into your day. That's one way to simplify—to schedule time to do nothing, so you won't be overscheduled. This leaves room for those meetings that run late, people who don't show up to or leave from their appointments on time, unexpected delays, and unexpected demands that suddenly come up. For all those situations, it helps to have some open space planned into your day. How do you get that? Simply plan for it. Don't schedule appointments back to back. Give yourself some breaks in between obligations. By giving yourself some open space, you're keeping yourself from running too harried and you're simplifying your day just a little bit more.

Finding Contentment

I believe one reason our lives are so complicated these days is because we tend to never be satisfied. We want more options so we can be sure of having what we want. We tend to think, *The more choices I have, the more options available to me, the better the chance that I'll be happy.* Yet the Bible says, "Godliness with contentment is great gain. For we brought nothing into the world, and we can take nothing out of it. But if we have food and clothing, we will be content with that" (1 Timothy 6:6–8).

Oh to be content simply with food and clothing—how much simpler life would be!

The psalmist wrote, in simple sincerity, "You still the hunger of those you cherish; their sons have plenty....And I—in righteousness I will see your face; when I awake, I will be satisfied with seeing your likeness" (Psalm 17:15 NASB).[1]

The more content I am with just having Jesus, the simpler my day is. And the less I have to have. And the less I have to have, the less debt I accrue. And the less debt and obligations I have, the less stress I have to deal with. If my satisfaction is contingent on seeing God's likeness (in me) as He conforms me to the image of Himself while I am going through life, day to day, then the things that tend to run me down and make me feel like I'm running on empty will be those very things that cause me to be more like Him. The life-transforming process of becoming more like Jesus can be refreshing when I'm in the mind-set of keeping it simple.

Perhaps the best way for you to simplify each day is to look at it simply. And live it simply. The world will not stop if you do. Life will not end if you don't get the loan or the dress or the order exactly as you wanted. Stress is often a state of mind. Keep fresh by finding your open space, enjoying life, and keeping things simple. Many times I've streamlined an event simply to keep it simple. It still worked. It just didn't have all the bells and whistles. And few people noticed, or even cared, that it was scaled down.

As you look at your to-do list, or your closet of clothes, or your house to clean, or your project to complete, how can you simplify it? How can you make it more manageable? What three simple steps can you take today to make progress on it?

And don't stop there. Make a habit of keeping things simple, and apply this philosophy to everything in your life. You'll be amazed at how much smoother and less stressful life can become.

Pick-Me-Up Prayer

Lord, the essence of who You are is really quite simple. You loved me. You died for me. You rose again for me. You will live with me eternally. Forgive me for making the things of the Christian life so complicated at times. You are not the author of confusion, but of peace. And peace comes when everything is in order and when life is simple.

Take me back to the basics of what it means to rise in the morning, spend time with You, obey Your Word, and please Your heart throughout the day. And as I take my to-do list to You, help me to see how I can keep it simple and yet still glorify You in all that I do.

As I raise children, or work with others, or influence others around me, may I be a refreshingly simple person. One who can say what I mean with a few words, make a decision without a lot of fuss, get something done without all the complaints, and move on to the next simple thing. Help me to create those open spaces in my life so I can live simply and comfortably and without the added stress of being confined and crowded.

As I do what I can to simplify my day, I await Your part as You rescue me from the complicated chaos of life. And may I express, at the end of the day, the same gratitude as the psalmist did:

> *He brought me out into a spacious place; he rescued*
> *me because he delighted in me*

(PSALM 18:19).

Chapter 17

Take Time to Play

I'm leaping and singing in the circle of your love…
PSALM 31:7 MSG

Because you've always stood up for me, I'm free to run and play…
PSALM 63:7 MSG

Continuing on with our quest for simplicity, one way we can simplify our day is to take time to play.

Ever notice how children aren't usually stressed out? That's because they take time to play. Play energizes us. It keeps our creative juices flowing. It's an outlet of who we are and who we were meant to be. And there's no such thing as outgrowing playtime. Play is simply doing what your heart beckons for you to do. Some of us just need to remember *how* to play, that's all.

When I was a child, my friend and I made make-believe countries in the dirt in my backyard. No one was there to critique our project or tell us it was stupid. No one was there to tell us to be practical or remind us of what our project would cost. It was sheer creativity. We were playing by using our imaginations and throwing caution to the wind. And it was fun, and made for good memories.

What was play for you? Hitting a ball against a garage door with a piece of cardboard? Making piles of leaves and jumping into them? Dressing up dolls and taking care of them? Going outdoors and just running around? When we take our imagination, our sense of adventure, our competitiveness, our love for beauty, or whatever it was that got us to play when we were young, and we go out and *do* what our hearts are nudging us to do, that is taking time to play. And such recreation can help refuel us and keep us from running on empty.

Play to Ease the Stress

During my college years I survived the stress of a full load of classes (and a part-time job, as well) by playing in a women's community softball league. Granted, it was hard work. The game was mental, more than anything. ("Don't duck from that ball, Cindi, it's all mental!" my coach would shout.) But it was quite physical at times, too. ("*Run* for that ball, Cindi, sacrifice your body for the play!") The challenge to do something that was outside of my everyday routine (like sacrificing my body with scrapes and bruises just to catch a fly ball or to get on a base) was play for me. And the sense of accomplishment, of having played a good game, was exhilarating!

Determine that you need some fun in your life, and go for it!

Today, play is purely physical for me: hiking the hills, riding a bicycle, running around a lake, climbing to the top of the highest peak in some nearby hills, jumping around in my Jazzercise® class, or attempting flips on my friends' trampoline. What represents play for you? Is it exercising your mind through a good game of chess? Is it the challenge of a relaxing, calculated game of golf? Playing a board game with your child? Planning and executing a shopping trip? Creating something from nothing? Hanging out with friends? Find out what puts a smile on your face and makes you feel energized and exhilarated…and then make time to *do* it!

Ways to Play

Here are some ways you can take time to play:

- Do something you loved doing as a child: ride a bicycle, run through the sprinklers, climb a tree, or make up a game and get your kids, grandkids, or neighbor kids involved. If the thought crosses your mind that you'll look silly at play, get over it. Once you quit worrying about what others may think, you can play and have some fun.

- Join a community or church sports league. Unfortunately, sometimes these leagues become so competitive that they are no longer fun. But whether or not it's play is your own perspective. Determine that you need some fun in your life, and go for it!

- Take up a new interest. When my husband and I vacationed at the lake a couple summers ago, we played a few games of tennis. That was fun (even though I lost!). I hadn't played tennis in years. My husband and I still talk about finding some local courts and taking up the sport again. It was different, it was outside our realm of usual activity, and it was fun.

- Plan a party. Some women I know are really into this. That's because they recognize the value of celebrating. You can celebrate promotions at work, children's accomplishments, significant milestones (such as a child's first lost tooth, or a friend's new home), birthdays, anniversaries, holidays, and even life itself. Celebration energizes us. Sometimes we're just exhausted after a party, but it's a good exhaustion. Playing hard (with some good clean fun, of course) is good for our spirit. And it's a good change of pace.

- Play with your children or grandchildren. My daughter is 13 as I write this. And I have to really *push* her to play sometimes…because everything to her, at this age, is embarrassing. And everything her mother does is embarrassing. (Actually, kindly embarrassing my daughter is sometimes great fun— it's one way I can play. But I'd rather have her playing *with* me than have her look on in horror as I play alone.) Because children are energetic and much more prone to play, learn to respond willingly and positively when you hear them say, "Mommy, will you play with me?" Whether it's chasing them around a park, playing hide-and-seek in the house, or helping them build towns or dress up their dolls, taking some time out to play will bring important balance to your life.

Jesus Must've Played

Sometimes we tend to think that taking time to play is not "spiritual." Would Jesus have played? I tend to think so. Even though He is often called the Man of Sorrows, I bet He knew what it meant to play. I imagine He laughed with all the fullness of His heart and lived life to the fullest in ways that honored His Father. Yes, He had a mission, but I'm sure He knew the value of taking a break and enjoying time with others. When children came to Jesus, He embraced them.[1] Perhaps He even played with them. I don't think children would have been drawn to Jesus solely because of His great teaching. I cannot help but think they were drawn to His heart, His smile, and maybe His willingness to play with them.

The next time you start to feel run down and too busy to enjoy life, remember two simple yet important truths: Life is precious. And our time on earth is short.

Keep fresh—and keep from running on empty—by taking time to play.

Pick-Me-Up Prayer

Lord Jesus, how I long to know what it would have been like to see You play, to hear You laugh, to watch You enjoy life. Yet in heaven, I will be doing just that. Not only watching You, but enjoying life *with* You.

Lord, You must have known that through play, we can release the tension and enjoy life. And You *did* create us to enjoy us forever. Help me to take time to play, to make it a priority at the right times. May play remind me of how simple life is, how precious life is, and how short life here on earth is. And may it instill in me a greater longing for heaven—a place where I will enjoy Your company, and all You have given me, forever.

Chapter 18

Take Time to Reflect

My heart says of you, "seek his face!"
Your face, LORD, I will seek.
PSALM 27:8

One of my favorite stories in the Bible is that of Enoch. We don't read much about him. He's mentioned in only a few verses in Genesis. But what we read of him is extraordinary:

> Enoch walked with God; then he was no more, because God took him away (5:24).

Did you catch that? Earlier in Genesis 5 we're told that "Enoch walked with God 300 years" (verse 22). Altogether, Enoch lived to be 365 years old. But his father, Jared, lived 962 years. And his son, Methuselah, grew to become the oldest living man ever on earth. He died at 969 years.

Apparently Enoch and God had a close relationship. Is it possible that after Enoch walked with God for 300 years, God may have thought, "Enoch's dad lived to be more than 900 years old. I'm not waiting another 600 years for Enoch to be with Me here in heaven, so I'm just going to bring him up here *right now*"? As Scripture says, "…then [Enoch] was no more, because God took him away."

Oh to have such a sweet relationship with God here on earth that He absolutely can't wait any longer for us to be with Him in heaven!

While we cannot expect to be taken up as Enoch was, we ought to desire to walk with God as closely as possible for the rest of our life. To walk with God is to spend time with Him, talk to Him, listen to Him, commune with Him, and reflect on Him.

It's interesting that Scripture doesn't say, "Enoch *followed* God 300 years." Enoch didn't merely follow after God. It also doesn't say, "Enoch *served* God 300 years." That would imply Enoch was doing something *for* God. The verse says Enoch *walked* with God. It was a relationship. A togetherness. A communion. Enoch walked *alongside* God, not out in front of Him, hurriedly, yelling for God to catch up. Not lagging behind Him, telling God to slow down. Enoch took the time to walk *with* God—and he found a special place in God's heart by doing so.

Time to Start Walking

One reason we tend to feel like we're running on empty is because, as women, we're constantly running. Seldom do we describe ourselves as walking on empty or even sitting on empty. We *run* on empty because we run until we feel we can't run any longer and then we continue to run when we've got nothing left.

But what if we were to take time to reflect and commune with God, and walk with Him in the cool of the evening?

When we take the time to slow down and reflect on the day, and we involve God in our reflection, we allow Him to teach and transform us. How much we tend to learn in retrospect! If every evening we were disciplined enough to "walk with God," that would slow us down and cause us to contemplate the day and learn from it.

I imagine that when Enoch went out for his walks with God, he may have started out in a contemplative mood, reflecting on the day and sharing his thoughts with God. I suppose, too, that what Enoch received from God on those walks was far greater than what he had expected.

I'm guessing, too, that after Enoch's long walks with God, Enoch's face shone, much like Moses' face shone when he came down from a mountain after 40 days of being with God. And when you and I take the time to walk with God, to commune with Him in the cool of the evening, to reflect on our day and share it with Him, I believe the results will show on *our* faces as well. Taking such walks will help slow us down, bring us to a place of peace, and recharge our batteries so that we're no longer running on empty.

Make Walking a Habit

What will it take for you to begin to walk with God as a way of life? Not just rising early in the morning and spending time with Him to help keep your focus, but ending your day with Him as well, in a time of reflection and contemplation, to help keep your soul fresh? Since we were created for relationship with the living God, returning to that relationship regularly to reflect and learn is necessary for refueling. And because we have a tendency to run ourselves ragged every single day, we need to be all the more diligent about refueling with the Father in a time of reflection. Only He can truly restore and refresh us. And what better

> Your Maker has been waiting to take some long walks with you.

way to let that happen than by communing with the One who fashioned our soul and longs for our company?

As you begin walking with God, sing to Him. Bring your day to Him and lay it at His feet. Eagerly anticipate Him meeting you and sharing His heart with you. And as these walks become a regular part of your life, you'll find they are just as necessary to your soul as food and water are for your body.

Your Maker has been waiting to take some long walks with you. Keep your soul fresh, my friend, by taking time to reflect.

Pick-Me-Up Prayer

Lord God, what sweet times of fellowship You and Enoch must have enjoyed...and still enjoy! How I long to know that kind of closeness with You. How I desire to have such a friendship with You that You look forward to the day when I come to heaven.

Teach me what it means to walk with You in a way that keeps me close to Your heart and keeps my soul refreshed and refueled. In the cool of the evenings, draw me to Your side to take time to reflect on the day, on all You have given and all You have allowed to happen. And in those moments that we're together, transform me in such a way that everyone who meets and talks with me will know that I have "been with God." May I be one who has "been with God" enough that I am not too busy or too worn out to be with others.

Chapter 19

Get Outdoors

I will meditate on all your works
and consider all your mighty deeds.
PSALM 77:12

There's something therapeutic about taking the time to go outdoors.

Perhaps it's the fresh air that clears our heads. Maybe it's the sunshine that gives us a boost. I suppose that just by getting outdoors and looking around, we are reminded that it's not all about us. We are just one part of a beautiful story written for God's glory, and if we're not careful, we could miss the incredible landscape surrounding our small part of the big picture.

Throughout the Psalms, the songwriters expressed discouragement and weariness. They, too, felt at times as if they were running on empty. And in addition to saying, "I will" and determining a course of action to get them out of their slump, I noticed many of them simply went outdoors and looked around.

144   When You're Running on Empty

For example, in Psalm 77, Asaph was running on empty. He said,

> In the day of my trouble, I sought the Lord;
> in the night my hand was stretched out without weari-
> ness;
> my soul refused to be comforted.
> When I remember God, then I am disturbed;
> When I sigh, then my spirit grows faint (verses 2–3
> NASB).

Then Asaph talks about how he's so troubled that he can't speak. And he is discouraged that God appears to be silent. Then Asaph wisely declares, "It is my grief [or perception], that the right hand of the Most High has changed" (verse 10). And in an effort to change his perspective and begin seeing things the way they *really* are, he says,

> I will remember the deeds of the Lord;
> yes, I will remember your miracles of long ago.
> I will meditate on all your works
> and consider all your mighty deeds (verses 11–12).

At this point Asaph may have walked outside and looked around him and realized that there *is* a God, and He is not silent at all.

> The waters saw you, O God,
> the waters saw you and writhed;
> the very depths were convulsed.
> The clouds poured down water,
> the skies resounded with thunder;
> your arrows flashed back and forth.
> Your thunder was heard in the whirlwind,
> your lightning lit up the world;

the earth trembled and quaked.
Your path led through the sea,
> your way through the mighty waters,
> though your footprints were not seen (verses 16–19).

Perhaps at that moment, a sheepherder walked by with his flock of sheep. Or maybe Asaph scanned the horizon and noticed a nearby fold. I bring this up because Asaph suddenly breaks from describing the natural world and says, "You led your people like a flock by the hand of Moses and Aaron" (verse 20).

While we can't know for sure if Asaph was outside when the thoughts in Psalm 77 came to his mind, there's no question that when we step outside and look at the world around us, we suddenly gain perspective on who we are in God's eyes, how capable He is of caring for us, and how truly big a world this is.

Seeing God in Nature

In Psalm 19, David makes a case for God by describing what he saw all around him as he walked outdoors in the land of Israel:

> The heavens declare the glory of God;
> > the skies proclaim the work of his hands.
> Day after day they pour forth speech;
> > night after night they display knowledge....
> In the heavens he has pitched a tent for the sun,
> > which is like a bridegroom coming forth from his pavilion,
> > like a champion rejoicing to run his course.
> It rises at one end of the heavens
> > and makes its circuit to the other;
> > nothing is hidden from its heat (verses 1–2,4–6).

In recounting the delicate balance and details of nature, David is assuring himself and others that there is a Master Designer and we can see evidence of Him everywhere we look.

In Psalm 29, David again recounts the power and wonder of God by describing what he saw in nature:

> The voice of the Lord is over the waters;
>   the God of glory thunders,
>   the Lord thunders over the mighty waters.
> The voice of the Lord is powerful;
>   the voice of the Lord is majestic.
> The voice of the Lord breaks the cedars;
>   the Lord breaks in pieces the cedars of Lebanon....
> The voice of the Lord strikes
>   with flashes of lightning.
> The voice of the Lord shakes the desert;
>   the Lord shakes the Desert of Kadesh.
> The voice of the Lord twists the oaks
>   and strips the forests bare (verses 1–5,7–9).

It's as if the psalmist were saying, "Get outside. Look around. And you can no longer deny there is a God." The point I'm making is this: Get outdoors. Look around. And know that the One who made all that you see is able to take care of your weary body and soul and refresh you once again.

No Matter Where You Live

Whether you live in sunny California, where it is wonderful to be outside almost every day of the year, or the Pacific Northwest, where it is often damp, there is much to see and experience by getting outdoors. Whether you live in the humidity of the South or the dry air of the Midwest, there is much to be grateful for, much to inspire you, and much to take in. Breathe deeply of the fresh air. Appreciate creation. Notice the colors. Soak up some sunlight. (Yes, we're all aware of the dangers of skin cancer, but avoiding the sun too much for the sake of our health can actually make us Vitamin D-deficient.) And if it rains most of the year where you live, sit on the patio and listen to the rain. (Here in Southern California, I'd love to do more of that. Rainfall is so rare and special here that I love to watch it, get wet in it, smell it as it hits the hot pavement, and listen to it tap or beat against the roof as I fall asleep at night.) If you live where it snows or freezes or is just too cold to be outside, find your spot by the window and, every once in awhile, open that front door and breathe in the fresh cold air.

> Being outdoors in the midst of God's creation reminds me that life is not about deadlines...

When I feel as if I'm running on empty, I try to make an effort to go outside to sit in the sun, walk around a lake, do some hiking, or do *something* outdoors. Being outdoors in the midst of God's creation reminds me that life is not about deadlines, the stack of bills on my desk, or the laundry piling up in my garage. Instead, those are all byproducts of the curse we inherited from Adam of having to work for a living. By contrast, a good walk outdoors reminds me that I was created to enjoy this world with the Lover of my soul.

The next time you feel the walls of your home or office crowding in around you, the next time you feel so stressed you feel as if you're going to scream, get outdoors. Close your eyes. Breathe in the quiet. And meditate on all God's works and consider His mighty deeds (Psalm 77:12).

Keep your soul fresh—and remember why you're here—by getting outdoors.

Pick-Me-Up Prayer

Lord God, when I go outdoors and notice the birds in the sky and the leaves on the trees, help me to appreciate all You have made, and help me to slow down and smell the flowers, walk in the grass, and breathe in the fresh air. On those days, Lord, when I feel as if I'm running on empty, show me Yourself in what You have created on this earth. And just as You provide food for the birds of the air and clothes for the lilies of the field, how much more will You provide for those who love You! Give me the sense of rest and peace that comes when I go outdoors and ponder You. And please recharge my batteries by reminding me that every bit of beauty that I see here is only a glimpse of what heaven will be like. Life is no longer such a drudgery when I realize this is just the "test run" for a life of total bliss in heaven someday with You. Thank You, God, that this life is *not* all there is. There is *so much* more to come…and I can hardly wait to experience it with You.

Chapter 20

Find the View

I will see the goodness of the LORD in the land of the living.
PSALM 27:13

No matter where you are, there's a view to find, a sight to appreciate, a visual delight to the eyes that will transport you to a place of refreshment and refueling so you're no longer running on empty.

We often feel as if we're running on empty when we've been stuck in the routine, trapped in the mundane, faced with the monotonous. Experiencing the same sights, sounds, and sensations over and over again can drain us to the point where we feel we need the spark of something new to get us going again. That's why a drive through the country, a walk around the block, a change of scenery now and then can recharge our soul and give us the added energy we need.

For example, I love taking the coastal train route from Oceanside to Los Angeles. The view is marvelous, for the tracks run alongside the Pacific Ocean. I can see the waves lapping against the beaches, and frequently I am reminded that many people in the world live their entire lifetime without ever seeing an ocean. But the train route from Bakersfield to Fresno is not scenic at all. The backside of Bakersfield isn't too pleasant—trashy backyards, laundry hanging on clotheslines, old junked cars, and broken-down fences. But I've learned to look beyond all of that and find the beauty that *can* be found. The San Joaquin Valley sunset—in its striking reds, pinks, and golds—is breathtaking and awe-inspiring. And if I look beyond the broken-down fences and the clutter of junk in various stages of decay, I can see a breathtaking sight on the horizon. There is still nothing like a sunset in the San Joaquin Valley in Central California. What an amazing view!

Getting Creative

Although I live in the San Diego area, which is known for its beauty, the view from the balcony of my bedroom is that of a parking lot at a home improvement store. Not a lovely scene. It was lovely when it came to making the price of our condo more affordable in a town where the housing market was soaring. But it's not lovely if you're looking for a view. However, there's a palm tree near the bedroom window, just next to the balcony. If I look out that window at a certain angle when I'm resting my head on my pillow in the early evening, I can see only the palm branches against a sunset sky. From that perspective, I feel as if I live in a cabana on an exotic island. It may take some imagination on my part, but even living next to a home improvement store, I can find a scenic view.

What's more, my church is located in a strip mall. The church building is basically a renovated pet store building that became a sanctuary and our classrooms and offices. Going out the front doors, there's nothing wonderful to see—a couple of fast-food restaurants, a gas station, and a mini-mart. But if I look over and above those buildings, I see the Palomar Mountain range and an occasional seagull, which reminds me that I live and worship in a coastal inland community only 20 minutes from the Pacific Ocean.

Finding the View

What about you? Can you find the view from your living room window? From your desk at work? From your car on the way to work or on the way home? By looking for

Find the view.
Take in the beauty.
Breathe deeply.

that which *is* beautiful and ultimately finding the view, you can rest your eyes and your soul on that something beautiful and let it transport you to a place of peace, praise, and appreciation for God's creation.

To find the view, by the way, doesn't have to be limited to looking at nature. Maybe the view you need to see to refresh your soul is a mother sitting with her child on an old bus-stop bench. What went through your mind as you saw them? When my husband and I visit the Wild Animal Park nearby, we see many exotic animals. But for us, more exciting than anything else is coming across a wild California mule deer that just happens to make that park its home. The park personnel call these deer "freeloaders" because they're not part of the park's "inventory." But seeing these mule deer now and then, especially upon walking around a corner and they're looking at us straight on, reminds us that there are still a few wild animals roaming the little bit of undeveloped land that is left in Southern California.

Find the view. Take in the beauty. Breathe deeply. And realize that running on empty is often a state of mind. You still have wonderful sights to set your eyes upon and help you switch your focus, literally, to something relaxing.

Keep fresh by continually looking for—and finding—the view.

Pick-Me-Up Prayer

God, what beautiful sights You put in front of me, perhaps waiting at times for me to notice them. Those sunsets that scream across the sky for my attention, the dragonfly that hovers over the backyard pond, the smile on the face of the baby. Help me search these out so I can pause and reflect on the wonders of this world You've created for us to live in.

Don't let me get too busy, Lord, to notice the beauty all around me. Don't let me get too absorbed in my own life to notice life itself. Keep my eyes heavenward, where I can see Your wonders, and keep me looking—and ever finding—the views.

Chapter 21

Regain the Wonder

...I will meditate on your wonders.
PSALM 119:27

Listen to this...stop and consider God's wonders.
JOB 37:14

When I lived in Fresno during my college years, there was a radio station that played ocean sounds from 10:00 P.M. to 6:00 A.M. I literally fell asleep to the sounds of ocean waves and the faint cry of seagulls in the background. Talk about relaxing! It was like falling asleep on the beach without the sand and the salt-water smell! Now that I live 20 minutes from the ocean, I don't get to hear the sound of waves as often as I did when I lived farther inland in Fresno (imagine that!). Which is why I've invested in an ocean waves soundtrack, a forest streams soundtrack, and even a thunder-and-lightning soundtrack. The sounds of nature are not only relaxing, but awe-inspiring and wonder-inducing.

Life, it seems, should have been written to a musical score, and perhaps it was. As God created the heavens and earth, perhaps He was serenaded by the majestic sounds of heaven. All the drama and the grandeur of music and creation together is awe-inspiring and makes me think of heaven. I have a CD titled "Impressions of the Rocky Mountains" with music that is breathtaking—it helps to create mental images of majestic mountains, panoramic skylines, and tall forests. For me, it's not only mood music, but worship music because it transports me to a place of wonder and imagination, and praise and appreciation.

I think all of us had more of a sense of wonder when we were children. But we tend to lose this sense when we become adults. We get so caught up in the seriousness of life that we lose the ability to live with a sense of wide-eyed awe and wonder.

What It Means to Wonder

To live with a sense of wonder is to believe God can do the incredible, to see Him everywhere, to live with the anticipation that He'll come through, to be aware of the wonderful story that He's placed us in and to live it fully with eagerness and anticipation.

As you live from your imagination and appreciate creation once again, you will enjoy life rather than feel drained by it. Your anxiety will be replaced with appreciation, and your busyness with rest. Engaging your imagination and sense of wonder with life will slow you down and cause you to smell the flowers, notice the sunset, walk barefoot in the grass, breathe in the mountain air, and enjoy a birdsong.

To live with a sense of wonder is to be aware, every day, that life is a drama and your Maker is the main character. You are His beloved that He came to rescue and whisk away to a happily-ever-after. As we carry out the mundane routines of our everyday lives and we lose our focus on what truly matters, it's easy to feel drained by the pressures and forget that life is a beautiful love story between yourself and your Maker, an awesome adventure in which you live against the odds that try to destroy you, a comedy at times in which the strangest and funniest situations take place, and a meaningful drama in which there are life lessons and spiritual parallels everywhere we turn.

Call me dramatic. Or a romantic. But I find that concentrating on the love story of our life brings meaning to each day and keeps me fresh in my mind and soul. In fact, one incident that happened to me recently reminded me that we live in a drama in which God is faithful to come to our rescue, sometimes through the most unlikely means.

Recapturing the Wonder

I was driving home alone one afternoon from a speaking engagement a few hours away from home. I was on a long stretch of road with *nothing* in sight for miles around. It was beginning to get dark. I had several hundred dollars of cash in the car from book sales. And just about the time the thought crossed my mind *What if something were to happen to my car out here in the middle of nowhere?* I heard the sound. It was a knocking sound, as if something were falling apart in the engine. The car got increasingly harder to drive and began shaking and wobbling. I smelled a strange odor, too. I pulled the car over, walked all the way around the car, and then noticed, when coming back around the front of the car, that the front tire on the driver's side had blown apart. (It wasn't just a flat, this thing *blew* apart!)

I groaned and called my husband on my cell phone. He instructed me to call our insurance company's emergency roadside service. I did, and after about 20 minutes of trying to describe to the operator where in the world I was (there were no street or highway signs on this road in the middle of nowhere!), she finally told me I was 40 minutes outside of Barstow and a repair truck could be out to replace my tire in two to three hours. *Two to three hours!* It would be dark by then, and I didn't want to stay in my car alone out there just waiting. Besides, I *really* had to go to the ladies' room and there wasn't a place in sight! So I told the operator, "Thanks anyway," and called my husband and said, "I'm going to need to put on the spare tire...can you walk me through this?"

There I was, in my nice "speaking clothes" by the side of the road, a cell phone in one hand, and the other hand rigging up a jack underneath the car. I managed to get the car jacked up. But my effort to remove the lug nuts that held the tire in place...that was another story!

As I was tugging and pulling—and probably quite a spectacle by the side of the road—I heard and saw a white diesel pickup truck pull up behind me. There was *no one* on this road except me and this white pickup truck. A Hispanic man with a white cowboy hat got out of the truck and asked if I needed some help. I explained that I needed to replace my tire so I could continue my long drive back home. He took over and put the spare tire on the car, warning me that it was quite flat. Then the man walked around to the other side of my car and pointed out to me the silver tread coming through my other front tire.

"You'll never get back home on that flat spare and this bad tire. You might get another twenty or so miles, but then this one will blow, too," he said. (He chalked it up to a bad alignment that had literally worn the front tires down to their treads.)

He then pointed behind him and said, "I know the guy who lives in that farmhouse right over there." (I swear this was the first time I saw the "farmhouse"!) "If you want to follow me over there, I'll put some air in that tire and take you up the road about twenty miles to the nearest tire shop."

I told my husband, over the cell phone, the plan, and then got in the car and followed the truck to the farmhouse.

No one ever came out of that house. In fact, it looked like no one lived there at all. I stayed in the car while the man pumped air into the tire. Then he came back and said, "I'm concerned you won't even get to the tire place with that other bad tire. Why don't you follow me to the tire repair shop in case something happens?"

I followed him, and after driving into a shopping center (where the tire repair shop was located) that I would've never found on my own, I parked my car, got out, and went up to the man in the truck.

"Thank you so much for helping me," I said. "Can I give you twenty dollars for your time? Or at least some cash so you can pick up some dinner for yourself?"

He refused to take anything from me.

"Well, I don't even know your name," I persisted.

"My name isn't important," he responded. "Tony here will help you out with anything you need." And then he drove away.

A mechanic approached me. He was not wearing a nametag. I asked if he was Tony, and explained that my friend in the white pickup truck had said he could be of help.

Tony looked at the pickup driver, who by then had looked back, tipped his hat at us, and taken off. "Who *is* that guy?" Tony asked.

"You don't know him?" I responded. "He knew *your* name."

"I've never seen him before in my life," Tony replied.

Scripture tells us, "Do not forget to entertain strangers, for by so doing some people have entertained angels without knowing it" (Hebrews 13:2). To this day, I believe I was not entertaining, but being helped by an angel without knowing it.

Living in the Spiritual Realm

Thinking about that incident causes me to live with a sense of wonder. I live in a story—a spiritual realm—in which God can appoint a fish to save a man named Jonah, who otherwise would've drowned after being thrown into the ocean…and can assign a man with a white cowboy hat to drive up in a white pickup and help me out alongside the road when I might've otherwise been in danger.

> God has written a fascinating story that He anxiously awaits to reveal to you.

How many other times has God come to my rescue without me even realizing it? What has transpired in the unseen heavenly realm to assist me or get me where I needed to go?

That, my friend, is the wondrous world we live in. A world in which "our struggle is not against flesh and blood, but against the rulers, against the authorities, against the powers of this dark world and against the spiritual forces of evil in the heavenly realms" (Ephesians 6:12). We're living our own "Lord of the Rings" movie in which the good (of God, not man) will ultimately triumph over evil. And in the meantime, we get to watch— and live out—the exciting adventure in which "if God is for us, who can be against us?" (Romans 8:31).

What will happen in your day to help you regain a sense of wonder for the God who provides, who rescues, and who comes through just when you need it? What will you see that will give you a fresh outlook on life and help you appreciate all that you have been given? What will you experience today that will cause you to say, "Whoa…that was a God-thing!" I believe that every day, things happen to help us regain that sense of wonder…if we're intent on not missing it.

The Story Is Yours

So, my friend, if you are tired and worn out and weary, would your heart come alive just by knowing you are living in a drama in which the God of the Universe will triumph over everything in this world that has gone awry? Will you get that extra motivation to get through the day knowing that the God of Wonders has you on His heart?

The story is yours to live. And whether it's a tiring, boring monologue or a thrilling, suspenseful story is really up to you. God has written a fascinating story that He anxiously awaits to reveal to you. Will you rise each morning and ask God to reveal to you His wonders and His ways in the story of your life that He has written out ahead of you? Will you look for glimpses of paradise in everything around you, and signs of His love in what He's created and what He brings your way? Will you look to Him to be your Hero, your Provider, your Knight in Shining Armor and then begin to see life as the adventure that it is?

The key to it all is to keep your soul fresh by regaining a sense of wonder.

Pick-Me-Up Prayer

God of Wonders, You own it all—the cattle on a thousand hills, the riches of heaven, the many wonders of the world. How amazing that I can live in the drama of it all! Lord, when I start to feel weary, remind me that You are not only in control, but You have an adventure for me to live. To know that I live in a spiritual realm where You are arranging the circumstances in my life to rescue me, come through for me, and dazzle me with Your greatness is a story so exciting. May that lift my spirits and give me the added motivation to see today as new and fresh and exciting when lived in the awareness of who You are and what You may do. Restore to me that wide-eyed sense of awe and wonder that I once had as a child. May I believe, once again, that I have a God who can do anything. And may I look at life differently today…through the perspective of knowing personally the all-sufficient and all-powerful God of Wonders.

Chapter 22

Re-ignite the Flame

You, O LORD, keep my lamp burning...
PSALM 18:28

Do you remember the thrill of falling in love? Was there a bounce in your step? A sparkle in your eye? A motivation and energy to do *anything* that came along?

And do you now feel locked into the drudgery of complacency—the monotony of day-to-day life? Oh, to feel like we once did when we fell in love!

The feeling of being in love is powerful. And powerfully motivating. Being *in love* is a feeling. But *love* is a choice. Yet you and I can make the choice to be in love all over again. How long has it been since you've had that bounce in your step and that sparkle in your eye when it came to your love life with God?

My husband, Hugh, recently taught a Bible college class on the writings of the apostle John. John was called the "beloved disciple"—the one whom Jesus loved. And if you look at his writings, you'll see that he loved Jesus, too. John leaned on Jesus' breast at dinner, he spoke up and asked Jesus things when everyone else was afraid to address Him. John lived out the last days of his life in exile, growing in his passion for his Lord. His words, at the close of the New Testament, show where his heart was: "Come, Lord Jesus." He was heartsick for his risen Lord, for the One he loved. I, too, want to live with the plea, "Come, Lord Jesus"... not because I want to get away from this world, but because I want to be in His arms, see Him face to face, and know Him as He really is.

As Hugh was teaching through John, he also preached through John at our church Sunday mornings. And in one sermon, Hugh talked about the things we do for love. He gave examples of some of the crazy, unexplainable, and often irrational things people do for the sake of "love." Running away to get married. Leaving all they have for the one they want to be with. Having a baby to save a marriage. Crimes of passion. Waiting years for one to get out of jail. People are willing to do such things for what they believe is "love" (but is often really a dysfunctional, co-dependent relationship). Then Hugh put forth this question to the congregation, myself included: What crazy, unexplainable things are *you* willing to do for God simply because you're "in love" with Him?

That question convicted my heart. I remember the days when I did "crazy things" simply because I loved God and wanted more of Him. I was hot in my passion for the Lord. And those were the days that I was fueled by my love for Him in everything I did.

How things can change through time.

A Glimpse of God's Heart

When our passion for God wanes, and the flame that once burned brightly begins to flicker, Jesus is the One who notices.

Our passion for Him is close to His heart. It's so close to His heart and so important to Him that He addresses it in the last book of the Bible. Some of Jesus' parting words to us, in Revelation 2, are a prophetic warning to the churches about what Jesus doesn't want to have to say about us.

In talking to the church in Ephesus (that awesome group of people called the Ephesians, to whom Paul wrote about spiritual warfare and the importance of standing firm in their faith as they were living in a pagan city and being shining lights for Christ), Jesus says this:

> I know your deeds, your hard work and your perseverance. I know that you cannot tolerate wicked men, that you have tested those who claim to be apostles but are not, and have found them false. You have persevered and have endured hardships for my name, and have not grown weary (verses 2–3).

It sounds pretty impressive, doesn't it? Jesus is saying, "I know all the great things you've done for Me."

But look at the next verse. Here comes the rebuke:

> Yet I hold this against you: You have forsaken your first love (verse 4).

Jesus is sternly warning that all our work and service for God means nothing if we've forgotten why we do it and for whom. In fact, our work for Him means nothing if we no longer love Him above everything else. Look at what He goes on to say:

> Remember the height from which you have fallen! Repent and do the things you did at first (verse 5).

Jesus is saying, "I remember the great love you once had for Me. You were passionate about Me. You remembered Me in all you did. You were motivated by your love for Me. Now look at where you are. You were once high on Me, but now look at *the height from which you have fallen.*" Then Jesus tells the people to repent and "do the things you did at first."

What were the things you used to do for God? What did you once do for Him just for the sake of love? What was it you did "at first," when you first came to know Him and love Him? Those are the things Jesus wants us to keep doing for Him so we can be refueled and refreshed, instead of going through the motions and running on empty.

I've been married nearly 20 years. And in the seventh year of my marriage I remember pleading with my husband to "do the things you did at first." It seemed the romance was gone, the passion was gone, the specialness of our relationship was gone. He claimed to not feel any differently about me than he did on the day we married. But I felt things were not as special, not as passionate, because he wasn't doing "the things he did at first." I couldn't put my finger on what those things were. I just wasn't feeling that the flame was still burning in his heart for me.

Imagine how Jesus feels when He sees our flame of love begin to flicker. "Repent and do the things you did at first," He pleads.

Hot or Cold?

In the next chapter of Revelation, Jesus again speaks about our passion—or rather, our lack of passion for Him. In His letter to the church in Laodicea, He tells the people, "I know your deeds...." But then He says: "...you are neither cold nor hot. I wish you were either one or the other! So, because you are lukewarm—neither hot nor cold—I am about to spit you out of my mouth" (verses 15–16).

Here again Jesus addresses our passion for Him. But interestingly, when speaking neither cold nor hot, He says, "I wish you were *either one or the other.*" Could Jesus be saying that He'd rather have us not know Him at all than to live as if His love makes no difference in our lives?

I believe Jesus is saying, "Burn brightly in your passion for Me… or don't claim to know Me at all." Wow! That is so convicting. And so heartbreaking. That passage is a prophetic warning to those who are in the church, and I would never want Him to say that to me.

Restoring the Passion

So, how can we make sure that our passion for Him never wanes? How can you and I put ourselves in a position where He can re-ignite the flame in our hearts?

1. Pray for Passion

The Bible says, "There is no one righteous, not even one…no one who seeks God" (Romans 3:10). It is not in us to desire God the way we should. A passionate love for Him can only come from Him and His Spirit's work in our life. Go to God and say, "God, I cannot possibly love You the way You want me to, but I long to…so would You put in me a passion for You and stoke the flame of love for You in my heart?"

2. Believe You Will Receive It

Once you pray for passion, believe you will receive it. The Bible says, "If we ask anything according to his will, he hears us. And if we know that he hears us—whatever we ask—we know that we have what we asked of him" (1 John 5:14–15). In other words,

> Burn brightly, my friend, and may your flame for Him never flicker.

since we know that asking for a passion for our Lord is something God wants to give us anyway, we can be confident we'll receive it. So ask away when it comes to passion, my friend. "And all things you ask in prayer, believing, you will receive."[1]

What are *you* willing to do for the sake of love? Are you desperate for our Lord? Will you press on for Him? Ask Him to stir that flame of passion in your heart once again.

To be lukewarm for God is to be complacent in our relationship with Him—to live in the drudgery of the status quo. But to work every day at keeping the relationship alive is to bring excitement to the "marriage" relationship with God once again. Will you put yourself in that place where He can re-ignite the flame of passion in your life and let you live for Him again?

Burn brightly, my friend, and may your flame for Him never flicker. And may you never again find yourself running on empty.

Re-igniting the
Flame Through Prayer

Jesus, how I long to love You the way You desire me to. How I want to go through each day with a song in my heart and a spring in my step and a sparkle in my eye simply because I'm in love with You. Yet busyness rushes in to compete with my time for You. Other loves so swiftly steal my heart away. And I find myself looking fondly on days past and the flame that used to burn brightly for You. Take me back to those days when a love for You stirred in my heart and welled up in my soul and I was shaken to the core by the very thought of who You are. Draw me to Your side once again and re-ignite that fire in my heart for You.

Help me to do the things I did at first, coming to You first with everything, putting You first in all I do, telling everyone of my love for You, singing to You throughout the day. I never want You to look at my life and say, "She *used* to really love me with a fervor." How I want You to be able to say, even now, "She is a woman who is motivated in all she does by a growing love for Me."

May I long for You as David did in the Desert of Judah:

> God—you're my God!
>> I can't get enough of you!
> I've worked up such hunger and thirst for God,
>> traveling across dry and weary deserts.
> So here I am in the place of worship, eyes open,
>> drinking in your strength and glory.
> In your generous love I am really living at last!
>
> (PSALM 63:1–2 MSG).

Welcome to a New Way of Life

You made it, my friend, through the pages of a book that hopefully encouraged you to find that energy and motivation to get through your day. But may I share with you the inspiration behind this book as well as the fact that I have not yet learned all its lessons myself?

Isaiah 50:4 says: "The Sovereign Lord has given me his words of wisdom, so that I know what to say to all these weary ones. Morning by morning he wakens me and opens my understanding to his will" (NLT).

I posted that verse next to my computer, where I would be sure to see it every day as I wrote this book. Those words from Isaiah were to encourage me, inspire me, and keep me going as I wrote with the goal of encouraging you and others who feel they are running on empty. Yet, dear reader, please understand that the lessons and words of wisdom contained herein have been written for me, as well as for you. I have by no means arrived at the place where I never feel run down and tired. To the contrary, I have learned alongside you what it means to keep focus, keep fit, and keep fresh so that together we can practice a new way of life—one of trust and rest, not of stress and emptiness.

This is not the kind of book where I expect that you—and I—have learned it all and have finally arrived. I'm sure there will still be days when we begin to feel we're running on empty. And on those days, you and I may want to revisit these pages in order to remember some of the simple truths of keeping focus, keeping fit, and keeping fresh. And I believe that staying in the place where God can constantly infuse His energy into us involves a daily process of going to Him and saying, "Today, by Your grace and with Your help, I will live my life differently."

Through this book I hope to have given you help you can use no matter how life's circumstances change. And I hope the book's message will encourage you to turn to the only One who can refuel you and keep you refreshed through all the seasons and stages of your life.

May you experience those "times of refreshing" and hear those "songs of deliverance" every time you call out to your Maker for the fuel that only He can provide.

Welcome to a new way of life, my friend. A way of life in which we *know* where the answer is because we know the One who *is* the Answer. May He, Jesus, continue to instill in you a passion for Himself, a purpose in life, and a zest for living so that you never again feel that you're running on empty. May you, instead, feel His support beneath you as you soar to new heights.

The Lord bless you, my friend, as you "mount up with wings like eagles" (Isaiah 40:31 NASB).

Appendix

Praying Through the Psalms

Praying through God's Word involves taking passages of Scripture and praying them back to God. Because all Scripture was inspired by God (2 Timothy 3:16), to pray God's Word back to Him is to pray "according to His will" (1 John 5:14).

Because the Psalms are songs of emotion, they are—in my opinion—the easiest portion of Scripture to "pray through." Below is a suggested process and an example of praying through a psalm.

1. Read one verse at a time.

2. Say that verse back to God as a prayer in your own words, saying whatever the Holy Spirit might bring to your mind. (You can use each verse as a praise, a thanks, or a request.)

3. Repeat this process to the end of the psalm, then proceeding in prayer as the Spirit leads.

Here is an example of praying through the first three verses of Psalm

1. The verse is listed first, as it appears in the Bible, then prayed back in my own words (there is no right or wrong way to pray back verses of Scripture):

Verse 1:

> Blessed is the man
>   who does not walk in the counsel of the wicked
> or stand in the way of sinners
>   or sit in the seat of mockers.

My response:

> Lord, You say that the one who doesn't accustom him-self to taking worldly advice, or hang out with sinners or make it a lifestyle to mock and gossip, is the one who is blessed and content. Help me to be the kind of person who doesn't associate with or act the same way as those who have no regard for You.

Verse 2:

> But his delight is in the law of the LORD,
>   and on his law he meditates day and night.

My response:

> Instead, may I be one who delights in Your command-ments and keeps Your Word foremost in my thoughts all day. May Your words keep coming back to me throughout the day and may they be still going through my mind as I lay down to sleep at night.

Verse 3:

> He is like a tree planted by streams of water,
>   which yields its fruit in season
> and whose leaf does not wither.
>   Whatever he does prospers.

My response:

> Lord, make me like a tree planted firmly by Your stream
> of water, yielding the fruit of Your character (love, joy,
> peace, patience, kindness, goodness, faithfulness, gen-
> tleness and self control—Galatians 5:22–23). As I dwell
> on You, don't allow me to become weak and frail, but
> instead, enable me to be successful because I've made You
> and Your commands a priority in my life.

Why don't you open your Bible to a psalm and begin practicing
right now? What's wonderful about praying through the Psalms is that
it not only refuels and refreshes you, but it gives you a tool that enables
you to help refuel and refresh others as you share with them what it
means to pray through the Psalms.

Notes

Finding a Way to Refuel

1. Niles, Henry "15 Signs of Burnout and How to Help You Avoid It." Taken from the Web site Assessment. com (Motivational Appraisal of Personal Potential).

2. Verses 11–12, emphasis added.

Chapter 1—Start Your Day with Prayer

1. First Peter 5:7 NLT.

2. Philippians 4:6–7 NLT.

3. Psalm 27:4–5 NLT.

4. Psalm 55:6–8 NLT.

5. For more on listening to God, see the chapter "Listening to His Loving Voice" in my book *Letting God Meet Your Emotional Needs* (Eugene, OR: Harvest House Publishers, 2000).

Chapter 2—Refuel with God's Word

1. Matthew 4:4.

Chapter 6—Act on Facts, Not Feelings

1. The hymn in mind here is Helen H. Lemmel's, "Turn Your Eyes Upon Jesus," copyright 1922. Copyright renewal 1950 by H.H. Lemmel. Singspiration, Inc.

Chapter 7—Determine Whom You'll Trust

1. "You Alone," © 2004 by Kristi Foss, on her "More than a Dream" CD. Used by permission. To hear the song, go to Kristi's Web site at www.kristifoss.com.

Chapter 9—Keep Godly Company

1. First Corinthians 15:33 NASB.

2. Proverbs 27:17.

Chapter 10—Keep a Healthy Diet

1. Pamela Smith, *Eat Well, Live Well* (Lake Mary, FL: Creation House, 1992), p. 55.

2. Ibid., p. 55.

3. "11 Ways to Find Your Energy," *USA Weekend*, September 16-18, 2005, pp. 6-11.

4. This information is based on principles found in Susan Lark, M.D. *The Chemistry of Success: Six Secrets of Peak Performance* (San Francisco: Bay Books, 1999).

Chapter 12—Keep Your Sleep

1. Information based on "11 Ways to Find Your Energy," *USA Weekend*, September 16-18, 2005, p. 6.

Chapter 13—Keep at It

1. This is found in 1 Kings 18–19:12.

Chapter 16—Regain the Wonder

1. Psalm 17:15.

Chapter 17—Take Time to Play

1. Matthew 19:13–14.

Chapter 22—Re-ignite the Flame

1. Matthew 21:22 NASB.

An Invitation to Write

How has God refueled and refreshed your soul through this book? Cindi would love to hear from you and know how you've been ministered to or encouraged through her writing. You can contact her online at Cindispeaks@msn.com, or write:

Cindi McMenamin
c/o Harvest House Publishers
990 Owen Loop North
Eugene, OR 97402–9173

If you would like Cindi to speak to your group, you can contact her and receive more information about her speaking ministry at www.cindispeaks.com.

Other Books by
Cindi McMenamin

When Women Walk Alone

Whether you feel alone from being single, facing challenging life situations, or from being the spiritual head of your household, discover practical steps to finding support, transforming loneliness into spiritual growth, and turning your alone times into life-changing encounters with God.

Letting God Meet Your Emotional Needs

Discover true intimacy with God in this book that shows how to draw closer to the lover of your soul and find that He can, indeed, meet your deepest emotional needs.

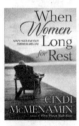

When God Pursues a Woman's Heart

Recapture the romance of a relationship with God as you discover the many ways God loves you and pursues your heart as your hero, provider, comforter, friend, valiant knight, loving Daddy, perfect prince, and more.

When Women Long for Rest

When Women Long for Rest is an invitation for women to find their quiet place at God's feet—a place where they can listen to Him, open their hearts to Him, and experience true rest.

When a Women Discovers Her Dream

It's never too late for a woman to discover and live out her dreams in life. Explore God's purpose for you, and make greater use of your uniqueness and special gifts.